EFFECTIVE COMMUNICATION

FOR PROFESSIONALS

DONALD J. SHIELDS
with
LELA K. BULLERDICK / DONALD G. SHIELDS

Advanced Communication Training Seminars

KENDALL/HUNT PUBLISHING COMPANY
2460 Korper Boulevard P.O. Box 539 Dubuque, Iowa 52004-0539

Cover illustration: BISMARCK ADDRESSING THE
REICHSTAG
From a Painting by Ernest Henseler

CONTENTS

A Word about Ethics and Communication
in a Free Society

Freedom in relation to social and physical environment means *Effective Choice*. Man is free, only in proportion as he does, or thinks, or as he chooses. Most communication is an attempt to influence these choices. For a communicator to be ethical their message should allow this choice making to be voluntary and free from physical or mental coercion. It should be based on available information and include knowledge of possible alternatives and the probable consequences of the choice. The audience should be aware of the motives and values of the communicator who presents them with the choices.

Justice Oliver Wendell Holmes pointed out that our freedom as a nation can only be preserved in a society that allows for a "free market place of ideas". A society that allows all points of view, however, strange or repulsive, to be heard and discussed is the only truly free society. This principle is based on the assumption that every person has the right to make their own free choices and determine their own destiny.

Every communicator is attempting to affect their audience and their choices in some manner. If we are ethical communicators those choices we offer our audiences should be free and not coerced. A communicator must be willing to stand behind what they advocate and propose and be able to honestly say, "I believe that what I propose will have good personal consequences for those people it will affect."

Communication is an attempt to impart knowledge or logically verifiable assertions that are perceived to have scientific or survival value in our society. The ethical communicator identifies their motivations and allegiances while the propagandist attempts to conceal theirs. The ethical communicator accepts their responsibility for providing free choice to their audience, the propagandist does not. The ethical persuader is concerned with the truth of their position, the propagandist is not.

For our society to survive and flourish, we must have persons that are dedicated to being ethical, effective communicators.

CHAPTER 1

Competition Requires
Effective Communication

Success in the modern world of business and industry requires managers and employees that are effective communicators. **You are a communicator almost every waking minute of your life.** Studies show that you spend seven out of every ten minutes that you are alive and awake communicating verbally. We devote only 25 percent of that time to writing and reading. We spend 30 percent of our time to speaking and 45 percent to listening. Even a small gain in your skills in this area can dramatically increase your long-term value and productivity to you and your company. **Most of your work time is spent in oral communication.**

As a citizen outside the workplace effective oral communication allows you to be effective as an opinion-leader in your community. The citizen that can clearly state a point and present persuasive argument and evidence in an effective manner is listened to and believed.

People make favorable or unfavorable opinions of you and your ideas based on their impressions of your communication abilities.

Communication Model

All of your communication occurs within a specific context. *A context is merely the situation you are in at the time.* We formulate our messages and the strategies for delivering those messages in relation to the intended audience, and the occasion. We speak to our family and our business associates in different manners. We are more informal and open with our families and more formal and careful with business associates. We select different words and phrases for audiences that are familiar with the technical complexities of a topic and for the lay audience that has little or no knowledge of the field. The *context* includes the physical and socio-psychological factors, the immediate and historic factors affecting the occasion for the communication and the relationship of the audience to the Speaker, Topic and Occasion.

For our message to be effective, we must adapt to the context of the communication.

There are **five** factors in any communication context:

1. *The Source*—You as the speaker are the source of the message. You analyze the audience, determine the purpose of the message, encode the message into words and select the channel or channels for sending the message to the audience. You must be perceived to be a *credible source*—Knowledgeable, Trustworthy, Dynamic and interested in your message.

2. *The Message*—The words you use to encode your meaning are merely symbols representing your perception of reality and meaning. **Words do not have meaning—People have meaning.** The meaning of the words you select may be different for your audience. Take for example the word *love*. You may intend the statement "I love you." to convey passion and romance but your audience may interpret it to mean a platonic liking. *Always select word-symbols that convey the meaning you intend to the audience.* A second equally important part of any message is *nonverbal*. Clothes you wear, gestures you make, eye-contact or lack of eye-contact also communicate messages to an audience. One study indicates that over 50 percent of the meaning an audience perceives from a message comes from the context and physical delivery of the speaker; and, over 30 percent of the meaning comes from the vocal intonation the speaker gives the words. Less than 10 percent of the meaning of the message is conveyed by the words alone. *How you look and sound when you deliver a message tells the audience what you mean.*

3. *The Channel*—This is the way you intend to deliver the message to the audience. It may be in person using a podium and standing in front of the audience. It may be in a telephone conference call or it may be by the use of a video-tape or actual broadcast of the message over commercial radio-television channels. The channel you select will affect the type of message and your ability to adapt and change that message while you are delivering the speech. The speed with which the channel brings speaker and audience together allows for a closer and more complete interchange of messages between the source and receiver. This speed of channel transmission also allows many more messages to be exchanged at a higher time frequency. Channel selection can significantly affect the success of your message.

4. *The Receivers*—The audience is a specific group of people at a specific time. They are affected by their perception of the Context, Message, and the Speaker. *The objective of any communication message is to gain the desired response from the audience. Communication effectiveness can only be judged by the response of the audience.* The speaker must know what the audience expects from this situation, what the audience knows and feels about the subject and purpose, and what other basic attitudes, beliefs, and values affect the audience in their perception of this message.

5. *Audience Feedback*—Speakers must note and adapt to the response they receive from their audience. Effective Communication is a continually adjusting situation between the speaker and the reactions of the audience. *A speaker must be flexible enough to adapt a planned message to the immediate reactions of a specific audience.*

Effective Communication is audience centered.

Perception and Communication

Words and Nonverbal elements are perceived in different ways by different audiences and individual members of the same audience. For a message to be effective it must be perceived by the majority of an audience in a manner that allows the speaker to gain their purpose. The audience must interact with the verbal and nonverbal message. That means they must give *selective attention* to the speaker and message. But, the audience will also give *selective perception* to that speaker and message. For example when we attend a basketball game we have decided to give our *selective attention* to the game; but, the way in which we interpret the events of the game, such as foul calls, is determined by our *selective perception.* If the foul is called against our team we may perceive the referee to be wrong while supporters of the opposing team perceive the referee to be correct. Audiences react to words and nonverbal cues in speeches favorably if they perceive them to be consistent with existing attitudes and expectations. *The more you make your message seem consistent with existing attitudes and expectations the more likely your audience is to perceive it favorably.*

Communication Apprehension

According to the National Institute of Mental Health, severe "stage fright" is one of the most common phobias, affecting up to 4 million Americans. This Communication apprehension can arise in two different types of people. First, are those that are "perfectionists" who have an exaggerated fear of being scrutinized, judged and humiliated. This group is highly critical of themselves and imagine that others view them just as unfavorably, watching intently for the slightest flaw. The second type, are not shy as a rule. They may be perfectly at ease, even outgoing in any other social situation—as long as they are not in the spotlight. Some of this group are dynamic, and skilled performers. But, they suffer great anticipation anxiety: panicky feelings, insomnia and loss of appetite even for weeks or months before an event. This second group fear that others will perceive that they are terrified or out of control while they speak. Some in this second group may turn to alcohol or drugs to mask their visible symptoms and end up with an addiction.

The cure rate for public speaking phobia is extremely high.

One method is called *systematic desensitization.* In this process you are first asked to read a short paragraph or poem aloud while seated at a table with a small group of trusted friends or colleagues. Next, you may do the same while standing up at the table, then at a podium, and then with several strangers present in the room. Each step is slightly more demanding than the one before. At the same time you should concentrate on positive visualization of relaxed slow, gentle breathing, and muscle relaxing resulting in a successful presentation. Whenever any step causes too much anxiety, you are allowed to stop and relax until you are calm enough to try it again. Through this method, you learn gradually to cope with small amounts of anxiety and are able to take on more challenging assignments as your confidence increases.

A second method that can be used with Systematic desensitization is called *positive rehearsal*. This allows the speaker to practice a speech or report repeatedly before a video-camera or mirror until the material is thoroughly familiar. This method allows the speaker to be positive that they are in command of their content/message and by reviewing the practice video tapes be aware that their delivery has improved with the practice and that they do not appear to be ridiculous or silly in their presentation.

After using these two methods, on the day of the speech another self-calming approach is to fix your gaze on three or four people in the audience who look especially friendly and receptive. By trying to project warm, loving feelings toward these people, you will shift the concern and attention away from yourself and toward the audience. This method is a part of *positive visualization* where you concentrate on the positive reception and acceptance of your message by the audience.

To Overcome Communication Apprehension

- Take speaking before a group in small steps before small audiences one step at a time.
- Practice your speech using video camera or mirror until you are confident you know your speech.
- Practice positive visualization of the results of your speech.
- Select friendly audience members and talk directly to them.

Remember

- Effective communication is the difference between success and failure.
- Effective communication can be learned and improved.
- Effective communication is judged by the reaction of the intended audience.
- Effective communication is audience/context centered.
- Effective communication must be perceived as consistent with the existing attitudes and expectations of the audience.
- Effective communication results from overcoming apprehension.

CHAPTER 2

Who Is the Audience and What Do I Talk about?

As we will continually remind you—*Effective communication is audience/context centered and effectiveness must be judged by the reaction of the intended audience.* This requires you to find out as much as possible about your audience and their attitudes, beliefs, and values.

First: Find Out as Much as Possible about Demographics of Audience

1. *Age Range*—Attitudes and Beliefs tend to become more conservative in regard to social and economic issues as the age of a person increases.
2. *Sex*—All surveys taken in the last several years indicate that men and women tend to respond differently on many controversial topics. Women are more likely to support peace movements than men and to be more concerned with child-care and domestic economic issues.
3. *Social/Economic Status*—The social standing and power status of a person is closely linked to the amount of money they earn or possess. Many issues reflect the importance of this to a person's attitudes, beliefs, and values.
4. *Ethnic Background*—Is the person a first or second generation American, Black, Hispanic, or Jew? For many people their cultural heritage is very important to how they react to many issues.
5. *Religion and Intensity of Religious Belief*—Membership and attendance in religious groups has strong influences on many people. As recent political campaigns have demonstrated these religious affiliations and intensity of commitment can be the most important factor in some people's attitudes and actions concerning a wide range of topics.
6. *Special Interest Group Memberships*—For some people Union Membership, or Political Action Groups such as National Rifle Association, National Education Association, or other such groups can have a strong influence on their evaluation of major social, economic, and political issues.

Second: What Is the Audience's Knowledge Level on Your Topic?

What an audience already knows about a certain topic should help you determine how you can best extend on and adapt to that alrady existing knowledge. If the audience knows little or nothing about a topic then you must educate and inform them before you can ask them to believe and take action. It will also tell you how much in-depth technical terms and knowledge will be understood by the audience. If the audience already has a large amount of general knowledge concerning the topic you must adapt to that and try to *Take them beyond what they already know. Nothing insults an audience more than being talked down to by a speaker.*

You must know what the audience knows and adapt your message to that knowledge level.

Third: What Is the Audience's Basic Value/Belief Structure?

Attitudes—which are merely a tendency to respond favorably or unfavorably toward an idea, person, or thing—are all a result of our individual belief and value structure. These beliefs and values are based on things that we have been exposed to in the past and on basis of practical experience have accepted as valid and believable. For example we might have a positive *attitude* toward a proposed space mission to Mars because we *believe* that space missions help our country in both scientific, commercial, and military ways based on the past space missions we have accomplished. A belief is always consistent with at least one of our basic values. Basic *values* are common in most societies. They define our basic goals in life such as honesty, independence, intelligence, love, ambition. These are basic terminal values or objectives or goals we strive for such as, a comfortable life, a world of beauty, freedom, and equality. These *basic instrumental and terminal values are generally emotional in nature.*

These basic values and the attitudes and beliefs that are consistent with the values determine how the audience perceives our topic and purpose.

For the topic to be accepted by the audience they must perceive it to be consistent with these basic attitudes/beliefs/values.

You can find out what the typical American audience attitude might be concerning a multitude of issues by reference to public opinion polls that are conducted by such organizations as Gallup, Roper, and Harris. *For a quick guide to such attitudes/beliefs/ and values on current issues you can check the bi-monthly magazine published by the Gallup Poll:* **Public opinion**

Fourth: What Is the Audience's Attitude toward This Specific Topic, Speaker and Occasion?

Topic: Although you may know the general attitudes of the audience toward a general topic you need to determine the attitude of the specific audience toward your specific topic. Although they may be generally opposed to increased taxes they may be in favor of a tax increase for a specific educational or public works program they feel is needed. *If at all possible do a mini-survey of your specific audience concerning your specific topic and purpose.*

Speaker: Your reputation or lack of reputation with the audience will have a significant effect on their perception and acceptance of your message. It is true that the audience perception of **What the speaker is may speak more loudly than what the speaker says.** If you have an established reputation as a expert and a trustworthy source then you can use more personal examples and stories and cite less hard evidence from other sources and expect a positive response to your message. If you have no established reputation with the audience then you should cite authorities that the audience will accept as credible. This will help establish you as a credible source that is knowledgeable and trustworthy.

Occasion: The interest level of the audience can be significantly affected by the occastion. The occasion includes the purpose of the meeting, what has gone on before you speak, and what will happen in the meeting after you speak. If you are not the main speaker then your message must be adapted to the position you hold on the program—preceding or following the major "event" of the occasion. If the meeting is serious in nature then your message should reflect that serious purpose. If the meeting is casual then it should reflect that purpose. Abraham Lincoln adapted his Gettysburg Address to the Occasion. His remarks were to follow a 2-hour speech delivered by Senator Evertt of Massachusetts. The audience was standing in an open field under a hot summer sun. The purpose was solemn and serious—to dedicate a national cemetery to those killed in the Battle of Gettysburg. His remarks took less than five minutes to deliver. They were appropriate and solemn. *They will be remembered as long as our nation lives.*

Adapt your message to the occasion.

What Do I Talk About?

Your selection of an appropriate topic for a specific speech will be determined by the audience and the occasion. Now that you have determined who the audience will be and what the occasion is, you will select a topic that is appropriate *to you and your knowledge and interest.*

Most of the time, the topic you select will be obvious in relation to the audience and occasion. *The two situations that generally call for you to present a speech are:*

1. You are perceived to be an "expert" on a topic and are asked to speak; or
2. You are vitally interested in an issue or cause and you want to persuade others to agree with you or take action based on that belief.

For purposes of developing your speaking skills and practice you should try to select topics that: (1) You know something about and that interest you; (2) Areas that you want to explore and learn more about; (3) Areas that you can make interesting to the audience; (4) Areas that adapt to the occasion and social context of the practice session.

First: What Is Your Purpose for Delivering This Speech to This Audience?

This is the next question that you must answer. With this topic area and this audience and occasion, *what type of response do I want from this audience?*

- Do I want them to laugh and merely be **entertained?**
- Do I want them to gain new **information and knowledge?**
- Do I want them to be **stimulated (rededicated)** to ideas they already believe?
- Do I want to **convince** them to believe something they may not already believe?
- Do I want to get them to take **action** as a result of new knowledge and or beliefs?

What is the desired audience reaction: **entertain, inform, stimulate, convince** or **actuate?**

Second: What Is My Thesis Statement (Main Point) with This Purpose?

The **Thesis Statement** is the major idea you want the audience to remember when you are finished with your speech. It should be stated in a clear and simple sentence.

There are three basic types of thesis statements that can be made with any speech purpose: **Fact, Value, Policy.**

Statements of Fact: You assert that some idea, process, or procedure is true and has in fact been performed or can be performed. Currently scientists are debating the statement of fact as to whether a Star-Wars Defense system is possible. Other statements of fact that are the basis of much public discussion concern the possibility of successful space-travel beyond the moon into our own planetary system—i.e., Mars, Jupiter, Saturn and beyond.

Statements of Value: You assert that some object, situation, or idea is good or bad, useful or useless, beautiful or ugly. You are making a *Value judgement* and attempting to prove that the value judgement is correct and should be believed by the audience. Questions of value are different from those of fact. Once we had established in the 1950's the fact that space travel to the Moon was possible, we debated whether or not it was a **good or bad idea** to pursue the possibility of such space travel. In business and industry after it is established that the production of a product or service is possible we must next consider if it is good/bad, profitable/non-profitable, ethical/unethical to produce such a product or service.

Statements of Policy: You assert that some policy (action) that is not now in operation should be adopted, or that some policy (action) that is now in operation should be eliminated. *You are advocating that there should be a change from the status quo* (Things as they are in the present situation). In business and industry after it has been established that a procedure is possible and that it would be a valuable project then we advocate why and how the procedure can be implemented. *Not only is it possible and good,* **it should be done.**

Third: Narrow the Topic to Fit the Time Limit

All speech situations have either a stated or implied time limit. In most business situations you are given ten, fifteen, or maybe twenty minutes to make a presentation. Your audience expects you to stay within that limit so that they can stay on schedule. Even when you are not given a specific time limit remember **Audience attention and interest is limited by the duration of the seat of their pants.** As a minister once said "No souls are saved after twenty minutes."

It is impossible to say everything about a topic in your given time limit. Instead decide what element or elements of the topic are most important for this audience on this occasion and limit your speech to those aspects of the total topic. *Narrow the focus of your topic to the needs and interest of this specific audience.*

Remember

Who the Audience Is

- Demographic characteristics of the audience
- The audience's knowledge level on your topic
- The audience's basic value/belief structure
- The audience's attitude toward topic, speaker, occasion

What You Talk About

- What you know and care about
- What your purpose is—what audience response you want
- What your specific thesis is on this topic
- Narrow the topic focus for this specific audience and this specific purpose.

Audience Analysis/Topic Selection Check List

Audience Demographics

AGE RANGE: 0–12 _____ 13–18 _____ 18–26 _____ 26–40 _____ 41–60

_____ 60–75 _____ 75+ _____

SEX: MALE _____ FEMALE _5_

SOCIO/ECON. STATUS: (Family Income per year)

$8,000–12,000 _____ $12,000–20,000 _____ $20,000–30,000 _____

$30,000–40,000 _____ $40,000–60,000 _____ $60,000+ _____

ETHNIC BACKGROUND:

WHITE _____ BLACK _____ HISPANIC _____ OTHER _____

RELIGIOUS AFFILIATION AND INTENSITY:

MAIN STREAM PROT. _____ FUNDAMENTALIST PROT. _____

LIBERAL CATHOLIC _____ CONSERVATIVE CATH. _____

LIBERAL JEW _____ ORTHODOX JEW _____

REGULAR RELIGIOUS ATTENDANCE: _____

OCCASIONAL RELIGIOUS ATTENDANCE: _____

NO FORMAL MEMBERSHIP OR ATTENDANCE: _____

SPECIAL INTEREST GROUP MEMBERSHIPS: _____

POLITICAL ACTION GROUPS:

Organization:　#　members in Audience

Importance
Very　Somewhat　None

General Topic Area _____

Specific Purpose _____

Thesis Statement _____

Knowledge of Audience Concerning Topic Area

Very well informed: _____ Somewhat informed: _____

No knowledge: _____ No knowledge and little interest: _____

Audience Attitude Toward
1 Very Favorable　3 No Opinion　4 Unfavorable
2 Favorable　　　　　　　　　　5 Very Unfavorable

TOPIC AND
PURPOSE:　　1 _____ 2 _____ 3 _____ 4 _____ 5 _____
SPEAKER:　　 1 _____ 2 _____ 3 _____ 4 _____ 5 _____
OCCASION:　　1 _____ 2 _____ 3 _____ 4 _____ 5 _____

Attitudes/Beliefs/Values That Affect This Specific Topic

CHAPTER 3

How Should I Look and Sound?
Delivery Factors

First Impressions Count

Remember   Over 50% of the meaning the audience receives from a speaker comes from the context in which the message is delivered and what they see the speaker doing physically.

Enthusiasm Is Contagious   You must always appear to be enthusiastic and dynamic. Your audience should believe that they are *the most important people you will talk to that day.*

All studies indicate that when people choose a politician they want to vote for, it is the person they perceive to be most sincere and confident. They don't buy the politicians ideas—which most people do not understand; they buy the politician as a person they can trust and feel comfortable with.

Your overall image, **Your Personal Style,** is the first impression you give.

This Personal Style Is Communicated by

1. your manner of dress/clothing
2. facial expressions—including eye contact
3. use of space, posture, gestures, and movements
4. tone of voice—vocal inflection

Dress for Success and the Occasion

Clothing and accessories are an indication of your status. They tell the audience who you think you are and what you want others to think of you.

You must first determine what image you want to project for this specific audience and occasion. You should be comfortable with the image you are projecting and that image should reflect the best of the real you.

It is always good to avoid extremes in dress, unless you want to attract attention to yourself in this manner. Try to avoid the extremes of contemporary fashion trends. Dress in a manner that will identify with the basic attitudes and beliefs of your audience concerning appropriate attire for the occasion.

You may feel more comfortable and relaxed in a polo-shirt and slacks; but, if the occasion calls for a business suit; wear the business suit! You can still wear a bright accent of color even with the most conservative suit.

It does not matter how expensive your outfit. It matters that the manner in which you dress tells the audience you care for their opinions and beliefs. It should tell the audience that you care enough to present yourself at your best.

Look Like You Enjoy Talking to the Audience

"A smile is worth a thousand frowns." This old saying is **True** when it comes to delivering a speech. Your facial expression should be natural. It should reflect your spontaneity and sincerity. It should reflect the feelings you have for the message you are delivering. If you don't know what you look like when you speak, practice in front of a mirror. Better yet, videotape your practice sessions and review the video. This will also help to relieve communication anxiety. You will be prepared and know exactly what you want to say to this audience.

Eye Contact Is Essential

Our culture expects good direct eye contact. Eye contact helps to establish credibility and build rapport. Generally we do not trust people that will not look us in the face or have "shifty eyes." When you first start to speak it is a good idea to pick out two or three people in different parts of the room that appear to have a sympathetic expression. Then talk directly to those people. Notice how they respond and adjust your presentation to their responses. Gradually you can expand your direct eye-contact to other members of the audience around these two or three people. **Don't just look generally at your audience—See them—Notice how they respond—Have a conversation with specific members of the larger audience.**

Body Language

Use of Space, Posture, Gestures, and Movements

Any actor will tell you that using your body to depict an action or convey an emotion is what acting is all about. The same is true in Public Speaking. The only difference is that in Public Speaking you are depicting action and conveying emotions that are your own, not those of the plays author.

Use Space to Achieve the Desired Effect

Like the Actor the Public Speaker has a stage, a physical space that they must use in conveying the meaning, action, and emotion of their speech. Should you stand behind a podium? Should you move out in front of the Podium? Should you sit on the edge of the desk? Should you go out into the audience? The answer to these questions depends on your message, your confidence, and the expectations of the audience in that specific situation. *You should utilize the space available for the effect you want to achieve. Nothing is more boring than a static figure standing stiffly behind a podium.*

Posture

Your posture should be relaxed and erect, even if you are sitting. You should appear to be dynamic and enthusiastic. If you slump and lean on the podium you are telling the audience they can slump and not pay attention. You should keep your weight evenly distributed and your feet and any moves should be positive definite moves that contribute to an appearance of dynamic energy on your part. *Do not shift weight and sway behind the podium.*

Gestures

When you talk with friends you normally use gestures to illustrate and emphasize points you wish to make. Gestures should be natural and uninhibited. They should be expansive and easily seen by the audience. They should be definite and purposeful to help emphasize the content and emotion of the message.

Some Basic Things You Should Not Do

1. Use nervous non-definite fluttering or wringing of hands.
2. Keep your hands in your pockets throughout the presentation.
3. Keep your hands behind your back.
4. Keep your arms crossed.
5. Place both hands on your hips in an "I dare you pose".

Some Things You Should Do

1. Use your hands to gesture and help communicate content—not distract from that content.
2. Make gestures definite and forceful.
3. Make gestures natural and appropriate to content and occasion.

Movements

Movement attracts audience attention. Static standing behind a podium soon bores the audience and they lose interest. Even if you have to use a podium for your notes or for a microphone experiment with movements away from the podium. Try speaking from one side of the podium and then the other side of the podium. Move back from the podium. If you need a microphone for the presentation ask if a lapel mini-mike is available so you can move to the front of the podium and get closer to the audience. The podium places a physical barrier between you and your audience and nonverbally can set up a communication barrier between you and your audience.

Some Things You Should Not Do

1. Do not rock back and forth behind a podium.
2. Do not pace back and forth.
3. Do not do a nervous dance with your feet.

1. Make movements purposeful and definite.
2. Make movements relaxed and natural.
3. Make movements accent important points of your message.

One of the best ways to prepare for effective physial delivery is to practice your speech in front of a video camera. Watch yourself and see how you look to other people. Then go back and practice your presentation again, trying to eliminate distracting elements and increase items that will make your presentation more effective. Videocameras can generally be rented for a minimum fee. For major presentations the expense is minimal for the increased effectiveness it will allow you to achieve.

Sound Like You Enjoy Talking to the Audience

Remember—over 30% of the meaning the audience gains from your presentation comes from the vocal emphasis and inflection you give to the words you are using.

> **Your voice can be your most important tool.** But, first you must speak loudly enough to be understood and you must articulate clearly enough so the audience can easily understand the words. These factors of intelligibility and articulation demand that your pronunciation be within the acceptable range of general American speech and that your oral language be grammatically correct.

> There are three major variables you can control to achieve emphasis and meaning in your vocal delivery: **Pitch, Rate,** and **Volume.**

Pitch: No song has ever been popular that uses only one note or a very limited range of notes. Your voice will be more interesting and effective if you use the total pitch range available to you. You should experiment with your pitch range. Try to avoid the high pitched nasal twang and the low pitched guttural growl.

Rate: Our average conversational rate of speech is about 125 words per minute. But, when we are under stress we tend to increase our rate. This may not be a problem if your articulation is good and your audience is interested. Try to pace your speech so that you vary the rate. You can speed up at some points for emphasis and slow down at other spots for emphasis.

Force: Problems of volume should be solved in practice. **You must always be loud enough to be heard. But, you should not continually shout at your audience.** By raising or lowering your volume you can achieve vocal emphasis. Sometimes lowering your voice gains more attention and emphasis than shouting. It is important to practice in the setting where the speech will be delivered, if at all possible, to determine the volume levels that will be appropriate and effective in that situation.

Things to Do to Improve Vocal Delivery

1. Tape record or video tape your speech and then with your eyes closed, listen to the speech.
2. Try several different major phrases of the speech with different vocal pitch, rate, and force emphasis.
3. Vary your vocal presentation in some way every one or two minutes.

Forms of Speech Delivery

There are four forms or methods of delivery that are generally possible: Impromptu, Memorized, Manuscript, Extemporaneous.

Impromptu: This implies that there has been little or no previous planning or preparation for this specific presentation. But in fact, your whole life and career should have provided you with material that is appropriate for a short presentation on short notice. All you need to do is know how to quickly structure a small portion of that material for this audience. A handy formula for such an occasion is **PRE—Point, Reason, Example.**

- **What specific <u>point</u> do you want to make to this audience?**
- **What is the <u>reason</u> you make this point to this audience?**
- **What <u>example</u> can you provide that shows the point is true?**

We will return to this formula later when we talk about organizational structures for various types of speech presentations.

Memorized: This type of delivery is very difficult to make appear alive, enthusiastic and conversational. Unless you are an accomplished actor you should avoid this method of delivery. There is nothing more embarrassing for the speaker and the audience than to have a memory lapse in a memorized speech. *This form of presentation lacks the spontaneity and life that is necessary for a dynamic, conversational style.*

Manuscript: This method of presentation should only be used when the speaker is in a position where his words and mistakes in those words could have a serious affect on either the speaker, company that the speaker represents, or other significant interest. As with the memorized speech, *This form of presentation lacks the spontaneity and life that is necessary for a dynamic, conversational style.* Only two Presidents in the last thirty years, John F. Kennedy, and Ronald Reagan, have been successful in the use of this form of presentation.

Extemporaneous: This method demands total and complete planning and preparation. Generally, a full-content sentence outline is developed of the speech. *But, the actual exact wording of the speech is not written or committed to memory. Instead the major thesis, points supporting the thesis and evidence supporting the points is organized.* Every time you deliver this speech the ideas and organizational structure will be the same. *But, the exact wording and transitions will vary with the audience response and occasion. This method helps you maintain the original spontaneity and freshness of ideas. It also allows you to expand or contract certain points in reaction to your audience response during the speech. Generally it allows for a more natural and conversational delivery.*

> **How you look and sound can make or break the effectiveness of your speech presentation.**

Remember

- Practice your presentation.
- Use video and/or audio recordings to check your delivery.
- Don't be afraid to experiment with movements and gestures.
- Don't be afraid to experiment with vocal inflection.
- Be the best you can be—make your personal style work for you.

CHAPTER 4

How Can I Make the Audience Believe Me?

In all communication context the success of the speaker in gaining agreement for their ideas and inspiring confidence is determined by the audiences' estimate of the speakers credibility.

Research tells us that an audience estimate of **credibility** rests on three factors:

1. *Are you trustworthy*—are you honest and sincere?
2. *Are you competent*—do you have your facts straight and know what you are talking about?
3. *Are you dynamic*—do you appear to be enthusiastic and are you willing to take a stand on issues even when it is not popular? In other words do you demonstrate you have **"guts"** *and a dedication to your ideas?*

If you can demonstrate to your audience through your content and your delivery that you are credible you will significantly increase the effectiveness of your speech.

Audiences tend to believe a speaker if first, they are a credible source, and if what they say is logical and emotionally pleasing to the audiences' attitudes, beliefs, and values.

Audiences generally demand some form of proof to be convinced of the truth or falsehood of a statement.

Proof is anything which serves to convince the audience of the truth of your statements. It can be a logical argument supported by documentation and evidence. It can be an emotional appeal that identifies with the basic attitudes, beliefs, and values of the audience. Or, it can be merely the credibility of the speaker.

Ways to Increase Credibility and Prove Points to an Audience Through Content

Evidence

Supporting Documentation

To establish your credibilty and logical appeals you must use EVIDENCE. You may believe that a certain policy or action will result in benefits to the audience. But unless you can present some solid evidence that these benefits will probably occur all you have for the acceptance of this belief is your unsupported assertion.

Unsupported assertion does not create belief and acceptance in the minds of an audience.

There are two basic types of evidence/supporting documentation for any idea you present: (1) materials that clarify and explain, and (2) materials that prove and justify.

Forms That Clarify and Explain

Explanation: Explanations tell what, how, or why and are useful in demonstrating the relationships between a whole and its parts. It is a description that makes a term, concept, process, or policy clear or acceptable.

Questions to Ask Concerning Validity/Truth of Explanation

- Is the explanation clear?
- Does the explanation accurately reflect fact?

Comparison/Contrast (Analogy):   These generally compare or contrast something that is already known or believed by the audience to some object, idea, or proposal that is not known. You can clarify your point by either emphasizing similarities or by emphasizing differences between your point (idea) and ideas the audience is already familiar with.

Questions to Ask Concerning the Validity/ Truth of Comparison/Contrast

- Are the facts of the comparison or contrast true?
- Does the comparison of contrast disregard fundamental differences in the situations being compared or contrasted?

Examples: These are stories that include **WHO, WHAT, WHEN, WHERE,** and **HOW.** They are a narrative in detail of a situation or incident that helps to clarify and explain the validity of your point. For an example to do more than clarify a concept it must be **factual.** That means that you must be able to verify that it actually happened. If the example is **hypothetical** it can prove nothing, but it can clarify the type of situation you are talking about. After you have presented one or two detailed *factual examples,* you might increase the credibility of your point by referring to other examples in much less detail that would support the point. These brief examples are called **specific instances.**

Questions to Ask Concerning the Validity/ Truth of the Use of Examples

- Are the facts in the example true?
- Have enough representative examples been presented to draw a generalization?
- Are there other examples that contradict the generalization drawn by the speaker?

Forms That Prove and Justify

Statistics: Our society believes that if you can quantify and count something it must be true. In business and industry a great amount of time is spent in producing "hard statistics" on numerous subjects so decisions can be reached. Statistics are basically the examination of a very large number of examples and the reporting of that examination in a mathematical form. Statistics are not just numbers. Statistics are numbers used to show relationships among various items. They are used to demonstrate largeness or smallness, to show increases and decreases, to demonstrate rate of occurrences etc.

Questions to Ask Concerning the Validity/Truth of Statistics

- Are the statistics from a credible source?
- Do the statistics cover a representative population and a representative time period?
- Are the units compared in these statistics actually comparable?

Testimony of Fact: Is an objective description (independent of any judgement or interpretation) of *things as they are.* It would be testimony of Fact to say that the Sears Tower is located in the loop in Chicago,

Illinois; or, that the Indianapolis 500 mile race track is located in Indianapolis, IN at the corner of 16th Street and Georgetown Road. Almost all evidence that is admitted in a Court of Law is Testimony of Fact.

Questions to Ask Concerning the Validity / Truth of Testimony of Fact

- Is the fact from a credible source?
- Is the fact reported in its complete form? (Not a White lie—by the omission of relevant information)

Testimony of Opinion: is referred to as *conclusionary evidence*. This form presents the conclusions/opinions of some source other than the speaker. These conclusions/opinions are used to support and prove the validity of the speakers point. Opinions should always be based on fact if they are used to support a point. This form of evidence is a source interpretation of facts.

Questions to Ask Concerning the Validity / Truth of Testimony of Opinion

- Is the source credible?
- Is the source specifically cited?
- Is the source bias?
- Is the opinion consistent with facts?

Evidence and Documentation contribute significantly in establishing the credibility of the speaker and establishing the logical validity of statements. Evidence tells the audience that what you are stating is *true*. It tells the audience that you are *trustworthy and knowledgeable*.

Use evidence and documentation to increase the effectiveness of your message by building credibility and the truthfulness of your assertions.

Motivational Appeals

Audiences enter any communication context with fixed attitudes, beliefs, and values. If a speaker wants the audience to agree with the points in the speech, the speech must make some connection with basic needs and emotions that activate these existing attitudes, beliefs, and values.

The most common classification of basic human needs that cause people to think, act, and respond was developed by psychologist Abraham H. Maslow. These basic needs in the order of their importance are:

1. *Physiological Needs:* the most fundamental need for food, drink, air, sleep, sex.
2. *Safety Needs:* the next most common need is for security, stability, protection from danger: a need for structure and order and a freedom from chaos and disorder.
3. *Belongingness Needs:* the third most common need is for love, affection, being a part of a group, being accepted and approved of by others.
4. *Esteem Needs:* the fourth most common need is for mastery, confidence, freedom, independence; for the respect and esteem of others. This is a need for **prestige, recognition,** and **status.**
5. *Self-Actualization Needs:* this is the highest order of need. It is a desire to actually become what you want to be; to achieve your full potential as an individual and human. This is a need for *being the best you can be.*

According to Maslow the lower level needs—physiological, safety, and belongingness—must be fulfilled before apepals to higher level needs—esteem, self-actualization—can be used to motivate belief and action.

As a speaker you must look at the specific audience and determine:

• What are the basic needs of this audience at this time?
• What motivational appeals will be most likely to make the audience believe that my ideas and proposals will satisfy these basic needs?

Motivational Appeals visualizes and asserts that your ideas and proposals will help the audience achieve their needs.

Types of Motivational Appeals

Acquisition and Saving   Will help the audience make more money, acquire more wealth, save money on a purchase. (Safety)

Increase Status and Prestige   Will help the audience be more powerful, more "in control", more respected. (Esteem)

Adventure Will help the audience escape from the dull routine of daily existence—add zest and a difference to activities. (Self-Actualization)

Personal Enjoyment Will help the audience enjoy the good things in life. (Esteem, Self-Actualization)

Companionship Will help the audience gain friendship, love, affection from significant others. (Belongingness)

Creativity Will help the audience become a better person, more of an individual, achieve their full potential. (Self-Actualization)

Curiosity Will help the audience disover a mystery, a new idea, a new and different product. (Self-Actualization)

Tradition/Conformity/Loyalty Will help the audience be a part of family, group, religious, national historically rooted action or belief. Will allow audience to be accepted as a "part" of the majority or larger significant others group. (Belongingness)

Fear Will help the audience to avoid beliefs, actions, groups, or objects that can be destructive of their lives, health. well-being. (Safety)

Defense/Fighting/Aggression Will help the audience defend their rights, get ahead of the competition, avoid being a loser. (Safety)

Pride Will make the audience feel good about their actions. (Esteem, Self-Actualization)

Religious/Reverence Will make the audience feel that their actions are an extension and expression of basic religious beliefs and values. (Belongingness, Self-Actualization)

Empathy/Sympathy Will make the audience feel that they can identify with and put themselves in the place of less fortunate individuals or groups. (Self-Actualization)

Sex Attraction Will make the audience feel that they will be more attractive and successful in attracting potential sexual partners. (Phsyiological, Belongingness, Esteem)

Authority   Will allow the audience to be in control, to be the boss and in charge of the situation. (Esteem)

One single motivational appeal is rarely effective used alone. To create belief (emotional proof) it is necessary to combine several motivational appeals that will satisfy a basic need or needs of this specific audience.

Remember: Audiences believe what is emotionally pleasing for them to believe.

Logical Argument

Although audiences rarely test your assertions for formal logical validity they are more likely to accept your message if the message is rational and sounds logical.

Audiences like to think that they base decisions on logic and reasoning supported by evidence. It is important that you organize your arguments and reasons in some type of logical order to meet this audience expectation. You can utilize any of these most common logical forms of reasoning in structuring your points:

Reasoning from Examples

Inductive Reasoning

In this form of reasoning we draw a conclusion based on the examination of several representative examples. We find that in several past situations the company has found that when they produce a new product certain consumer responses can be expected. Based on these past cases (examples) we generalize that when we produce another new product the same response will occur.

Questions to Ask Concerning the Validity of Reasoning from Example

- Are the facts of the examples correct?
- Are enough examples examined and are they representative of the majority of examples in this situation?
- Are these significant examples that do not support the conclusion that is being drawn?

Reasoning from Generalization

Deductive Reasoning

This form of reasoning relies on generalizations, axioms, or generally held beliefs. Over our life we have observed many different situations (specific cases) and as a result of what we learn from this specific situations we have formulated generalizations concerning appropriate actions. We have discovered that education helps people gain better paying positions. Therefore, we have a generalization that "Gaining more education will help our financial success." When we see a colleague going back to school for more education we conclude that they will be more financially successful. This form of reasoning is often referred to as syllogistic reasoning.

Major Premise: Education contributes to financial success.
Minor Premise: Marion is getting more education.
Conclusion: Therefore, Marion will be more financially successful.

We gain these axioms/generalizations from everyday trial and error living. Once we have gained this experience we apply it to drawing conclusions based on the generalizations.

Some generalizations/axioms are universal in nature. Our society has taught us that certain values and axioms are always true. For example, *honesty is the best policy,* is an axiom that we are raised with. If your specific case (Minor Premise) and Conclusion are based on one of these universally accepted axioms you do not need to state the axiom/generalization for your audience to accept the validity of the reasoning. When you do not have to state the Major Premise you are using an **Enthymeme.** This Greek term means that the Axiom/Generalization is "in the mind of the audience." This form of reasoning is very persuasive because the audience already believes the generalization to be true. You are using their existing value/belief system to gain acceptance for your specific ideas.

Questions to Ask Concerning the Validity of Reasoning from Generalization

- Is the generalization true?

Your generalization may be based on insufficient experience and observation. If the generalization (Major Premise) is false or cannot be supported by credible evidence the logic of your argument is destroyed.

- Does the generalization apply in this specific case?

Generally more education will result in a better job. But, if the education is in a field with little financial demand this generalization may not apply in that specific case.

Reasoning from Sign

This form of reasoning draws conclusions (inferences) concerning some item or occurrence that cannot be observed directly from some sign or indications that can be directly observed. For example we observe bulldozers and other heavy machinery being moved into vacant fields near our home. We infer that a new housing or commercial development is planned for that site. Our government may note that the USSR is massing troops on the border of Poland, we also observe that there is labor unrest in Poland, based on these two observable signs we infer that the USSR may send their troops into Poland to suppress the labor unrest. **We use these observable signs and indicators.**

Questions to Ask Concerning the Validity of Reasoning from Sign

- Are there sufficient reliable signs to justify our inference?

Without several different signs we are often mistaken in our inferences. Many signs are merely circumstantial. Weathermen rely on reasoning from sign. We all know how often they can be wrong.

Reasoning from Analogy/Comparison

We like to look at situations that we are familiar with and then draw conclusions (Inferences) concerning problems or situations that are similar to what we already know. We know that the management and production techniques of the Japanese automakers has been highly successful. Many American firms have adopted these techniques and procedures using reasoning from analogy/comparison. They find that they are producing similar products and what has worked in Japan can be adapted to work in the United States.

Questions to Ask Concerning the Validity
of Reasoning from Analogy/Comparison

- Are there more similarities than differences between the two situations?
- Are the similarities used to draw the inference the most important similarities in the two situations?

Causal Reasoning

Cause-Effect

We have been taught to believe that events occur in a predictable, orderly manner. If the death rate is rising from cancer we immediately try to identify the "cause" of this increase. Early in life we learn that every action we take (cause) will have some consequences (effect). Because this form of reasoning is so common in our lives it is often used to organize persuasive presentations. For example, you might claim that by producing a new product (cause) you will gain a greater percentage of the market (effect).

Questions to Ask Concerning the Validity of Causal Reasoning

- Can you establish which is the cause and which is the effect?

Do higher wages or higher prices cause inflation? Does the use of drugs cause family breakdowns or do family breakdowns cause an increased use of drugs?

- Is the asserted cause sufficient to produce the effect?

Is kissing sufficient, in and of itself, to produce pregnancy?

- Did some person or thing intervene to prevent the cause from having its normal effect?

Certain actions by employees would be sufficient to cause their dismissal, unless a close relative in a position of power intervened to prevent it.

- Could other causes have produced the same effect?

Smoking in bed could cause a house fire; but, faulty electrical wiring in a bedroom could also have caused the same fire.

Ethical Proof Factors

Audiences listen to and believe speakers that they perceive to be ethical and credible sources of information and ideas. It is very important for communicate effectiveness to be perceived as an *Ethical/Credible Source*. By using credible evidence, logical argument and credible motivational appeals you will increase your credibility as a speaker. Several communication studies give the speaker some clear guidelines in the development of credibility.

Use of evidence will significantly increase the effectiveness of the speaker. If the speaker is perceived to be a low-to-moderate credible source by the audience, the use of evidence will significantly increase their credibility. If the source is a highly credible source with the audience the use of evidence has not significant effect in increasing effectiveness.

Use of evidence from bias sources will decrease effectiveness. Evidence from sources the audience suspects of having hidden or self-serving motives will decrease effectiveness.

Dynamic physical and vocal delivery will increase credibility. Good physical and vocal delivery can increase the perceived credibility and effectiveness of a speaker.

Presenting new information from credible sources increases effectiveness. New information (evidence) that the audience is not familiar with from credible sources increases speaker credibility and effectiveness, more than the use of old familiar material.

The use of logical argument, supported with credible evidence, and appealing to the basic motives of the audience creates acceptance for your ideas with the audience.

Remember

- Use relevant evidence to establish your ideas.
- Use motivational appeals that relate to the basic needs of this specific audience.
- Use logical arguments (supported by evidence) that have rational validity for this specific audience.
- Establish your own credibility as a source of information and ideas.

CHAPTER 5

How Can I Get the Audience's Attention?

Content, events, and people that demand attention determine action.

If you do not get the initial attention of the audience and then hold that attention you cannot achieve the reaction and results you desire.

The Hook

The *hook* is a statement or action used specifically to get attention. Every good advertisement and television show constantly dangle hooks in front of their audiences. "Who shot J. R.? Tune in the next season!" "You can become an instant millionaire!" "Will Larry Bird retire? See our next issue!" All of these are *Hooks.* Once a television show begins, the first thing you see is action shots. The producers take the most exciting parts of the show and place them up front to hook your attention and keep you tuned in for the rest of the show.

The Hook should not only gain the initial attention of the audience, it should also give your audience a brief preview of the message to follow and some reason why they should listen to you as a source on the message.

To Discover a Good *Hook* for Your Subject Ask Some of These Questions

- What is the most unique, unusual feature of your topic?
- What is the most interesting feature of your topic for this specific audience?
- What is the most startling and dramatic feature of your topic?
- What is the most humorous and funny feature of your topic?

If you can reduce each of these features of your subject to one clear sentence you have several good ideas for a *Hook*. But the *Hook* must lead to achieving your central objective and purpose with this specific audience. So, select the hook that best adapts to your specific audience and communication purpose.

Humor Is a Good Hook

The best humorous hooks are stories of your own personal experiences. They are excellent, as long as they relate directly to your objective and your listener, and lead you to the major point you wish to get across to your audience. *Be sure that your stories are funny and in good taste.*

Rhetorical Questions Can Be Hooks

This hook ask questions of the audience that they cannot answer with a yes or no response. They are designed to provoke the audience to think about implications of your topic. In a speech on the proliferation of nuclear weapons a speaker started their presentation with a series of rhetorical questions:

"Will you be alive six months from now? Will you be alive next week? Will you be alive in 20 minutes? It takes only six months for severe radiation exposure to kill. It takes only one week for severe radiation burns to kill. It takes only 20 minutes for nuclear missiles to reach your city and explode killing you instantly."

Quotations Can Be Good Hooks

Quotations that are unusual and not well known by your audience can also hook the audience attention. But, if your audience is familiar with the quote it has little attention value. A quote from Lincoln, "Four-score and seven years ago, . . ." would gain little attention. But, another Lincoln quote that says "I do not now believe, nor have I ever believed, that the black man is the equal of the white. The black man is inferior and will always remain so." would gain immediate attention.

Use of Examples (Stories) Gets Attention

We all like stories that relate real events about real people and real problems. An example includes *Who* was involved, *What* happened, *When* did it happen, *Where* did it happen, and *How* did it happen. These stories can be from our own personal experiences or from the experiences of others that we can document as true. To get attention they should be vivid and illustrate the major point you intend to make in your presentation.

Visual Hooks Can Be Effective

A political candidate that had charged his opponent with a 50% absence record on voting in the state legislature set a vacant chair in the middle of the stage at each rally and placed a sign above the chair "Rep. Nelson State Representative Seat. Just like new. *Used only 50% of the time*." Rep. Nelson was defeated in that election and replaced by the candidate that used this **hook.**

A Hook Should

- Get the initial attention of the audience.
- Direct that attention to your message purpose.
- Help to establish your credibilty as a source of that message.

The Bottom Line

Closure

The conclusion, bottom line, or closure of your message is just as important as the Hook. This is your final chance to get your audience to pay attention and take action on your message. It should be a specific request for understanding, belief, or action. To select the appropriate closure ask yourself, "What is the one most important idea I want this audience to remember and/or act upon as a result of my message?"

The type of closure you select will depend on the purpose of your message. If the purpose was to inform the audience you will ask for a clearer understanding of the material. If the purpose was to convince the audience to believe something, you will ask for acceptance. If the purpose was to get the audience to take action, you will ask for specific observable action.

The closure should reemphasize and summarize the major idea of your message. It should tie up the idea and hand it to the audience in a short precise statement.

Techniques for Closure

The Challenge or Appeal   This technique openly appeals for specific support or action. It challenges the audience to take specific action and accomplish specific goals. It is usually a part of any conclusion for a speech that asks for belief or action.

Using a Quotation   As with the use of quotations in Hooks, the quotation should be unusual and not overly familiar to the audience. The use of the same quotation in the hook and in the closure can be effective, if the quote summarizes the major idea and theme of your message.

Using an Example   If you can provide the audience with an example of how acceptance of your message has actually resulted in benefits in a specific situation you achieve a sense of reality for acceptance of your message and the belief or action that you are advocating.

The Closure of Your Message Should

- Reemphasize the major objective/thesis of your message.
- Summarize the major reasons for acceptance of this message by this specific audience.
- Ask for audience acceptance of information, belief, or proposed action.

Keeping Attention through Content

After you have hooked the initial attention of the audience you need to develop message content that will sustain that attention. Several types of content seem to gain the most attention from the average audience.

Reality and Familiarity   Talk about real events, real people, real situations that your audience can relate and identify with from their own past experiences. This works best when it relates what is familiar to new ideas, concepts or theory. It takes what is real to your audience and allows them to see the connections and similarities with new ideas.

Activity and Movement   Stories and examples that have action and vivid imagery get attention. Chase scenes in movies, action shots in sports events all demand attention. Also the overall organizational pattern of the speech should move clearly from one point to the next. *Remember brevity and clarity are virtues.*

Novelty   Stories, Facts, and Statistics that are unusual attract attention. Routine events are not news; unusual, dramatic changes and events are news.

Conflict   Fights—physical, political, economic, or intellectual—attract attention. If the audience can identify with one side in the conflict they will pay attention to events to see if "their side" wins.

Humor   Humor in the major content of your message can keep audience attention. **Nothing holds attention more than the use of relevant humorous stories that illustrate points clearly.** But be sure that the stories are funny and in good taste. Nothing destroys a speakers credibility more than to tell non-humorous stories that are in poor taste.

Material of Vital Importance   If you can demonstrate that your ideas have impact on the audiences wealth, health, employment, or reputation they will pay attention and listen. We are interested in things that affect us and our well-being.

Content that gains and holds the attention of the audience will result in action and belief.

Visual Aids Get Attention and Contribute to Clarity (If Prepared and Used Correctly)

Visual aids help to clarify complex information and focus audience attention on significant points you want them to remember. **Do not use visual aids to impress the audience or to avoid interaction with the audience.**

Preparation of Visuals

Visual Aids Should Be Carefully Prepared Before the Speech. Very few speakers can use a chalkboard or flipboard easel effectively.

Visual Aids Should Be Simple and Have Only One Major Idea Per Visual.   The less figures per visual the better. Dramatic totals are more effective and impressive than a long series of numbers that result in those totals.

Avoid Information Overload.   Cluttering your presentation with too many visuals and/or too much information reduces their effectiveness.

State Information Clearly and Concisely.   As with other information BREVITY and CLEAR organization are a virtue that results in increased audience retention of information and ideas.

Make Sure Your Visuals Are Large Enough to Be Seen by the Back Row of the Audience.   Visuals that cannot be seen are wasted. Instead of clarifying they frustrate the audience and make it less likely the audience will give you their attention.

Some General Rules for Selection of Types of Charts

- For percent comparisons usually use the pie chart or map chart.
- To demonstrate how items compare or rank a bar (horizontal lines) or column chart (vertical lines) is best.
- To show changes over a period of time. Column or line charts work well. To show frequency (the number of items in different numerical ranges) column or line charts are recommended.

Remember to make your presentation audience centered. Not media/visual centered. Let your visuals aid you in making your information clear and interesting; but, don't rely on the visuals to make the presentation.

Use of Visual Aids

- Practice with the use of your visuals before the speech.
- Check out the room and the equipment before the speech.
- With the exception of models, it is seldom wise to hold your material while you are using it.
- Place all charts high enough so that everyone can see them.
- Do not turn your back to the audience when referring to your visuals.
- When using models for the purpose of demonstration, have a table or stand on which to place the parts.
- Do not pass out material to the audience until after your presentation, unless the material is to be used during your presentation.
- Plan the visual presentation so the audience can see you as well as the visual during the presentation.
- Never turn the visual on or put it up until you are ready to use it. When you are through with the visual turn it off or take it down.

Practice with your visuals will make you more confident of their use and will make their use more effective in your presentation.

Remember

- Hook the audience's attention.
- Direct it to the major idea and content.
- Use material in the content that demands audience attention.
- Conclude your presentation and achieve closure of your major ideas.
- Use visuals to clarify ideas not as substitutes for ideas.

CHAPTER 6

How Can I Organize My Presentations?

Organizational clarity is the most important factor in making your presentation clear and persuasive. The organizational pattern you follow should be one that is specifically adapted to best achieve the purpose of your presentation. The best method to use for developing your organizational pattern is a detailed technical plot outline.

Outline Your Organizational Pattern Closely

A clearly planned outline is the blueprint for your finished presentation. No contractor will start building a project until they have a detailed set of blueprints. *No speaker should start delivering a speech until they have a clear organized outline.* First, you need to start with a key phrase outline. Second you take that key phrase outline and fit it into one of the suggested organizational patterns for the development of a presentation with the specific purpose for that speech. Third, you work the outline into a full-sentence-full-content outline. At this point you should practice your speech reading through the full-content outline and then revise as a result of your test audience suggestions. Finally you develop a Phrase/Word outline from the full-content blueprint for use in delivery of the speech.

Some General Rules for Outline Format

- Each major heading should contain only one idea.
- There should be proper subordination of supporting ideas to major ideas.
- You should use indentation of items to show their logical relationship.
- A consistent set of symbols should be used.

So that you can see how these general rules are applied to the development of a Full Sentence/Full Content outline we have included the following Speech Outline example:

Full Sentence/Full Content Outline Example

INTRODUCTION

    I. Have you ever noticed the little signs on
       the back of a lot of semi-trucks that say
       "this vehicle pays $5,500 a year in
       highway use taxes"?

A. Your first reaction is probably to feel sorry for the trucker and wonder how he makes a living.

B. Then, you might think, well, what does the most damage to our highways and roads--the obvious answer is semi-trucks.

C. Then, you might remember the rough inter-state you have just driven and feel that when you are paying over $200 a year for use taxes the trucker doesn't pay enough.

D. You would be correct.

PROBLEM STEP

II. Our highway and roads are being damaged and the drivers of passenger cars are paying most of the bill for repairing these roads.

A. This can be shown by U.S. Department of Transportation reports as published in *New Republic* magazine of June 13, 1983. "Car drivers are paying 110% for the damage they are causing to the roads. TRUCKERS, ON THE OTHER HAND, ON THE AVERAGE, ARE PAYING ONLY 79% FOR THE DAMAGE THEY ARE CAUSING. TRUCKS CARRYING MORE THAN 75,000 LBS ARE ONLY PAYING 45% OF THE DAMAGE THAT THEY CAUSE TO THE HIGHWAYS."

B. The Federal Government is now testing the possibility of allowing even larger and heavier trucks as much as 35% larger and heavier--to use our Inter-state highway system (Source: CBS Evening News, Nov. 17, 1983)

C. You might think that the gas tax that Congress and the State Legislatures pass should cover the cost and that this is only a few cents per gallon which we can all afford to pay.

1. This is not true.
   a. Since Congress passed the last gas tax increase they raised the load limit for trucks on the nations higways from 73,260 lbs to 80,000 lbs.
   b. That is a 9% increase.
   c. According to the Civil Engineering text, PRINCIPLES OF PAVEMENT DESIGN, this 9% increase in load results in a 42% increase in highway damage.
2. To pay for this damage the State of Indiana has only raised truck use fees 25% to pay for a 42% increase in damage rate. (Source: Dr. J. L. McKinney--Professor of Civil Engineering--Rose-Hulman Institute of Technology, Terre Haute, IN.)

D. AS A RESULT WE HAVE GAINED NOTHING IN THE GAS TAX TO MAKE TRUCKS THAT DESTROY THE ROADS PAY FOR THEIR REPAIRS.

SOLUTION

III. There are several solutions for this problem that you and I as American motorist face.
   A. One solution would be to force trucks to carry lighter loads.
      1. A 40,000 lb load limit for trucks would reduce the pavement damage done by trucks carrying 80,000 lb by 92% (Source: Principles of Pavement Design)
      2. This solution is uneconomical because the whole trucking industry would have to restructure due to the fact that current equipment would be highly inefficient due to less load carried in a high capability load-bearing vehicle.

B. Another solution is higher road use taxes for trucks.
   1. This solution is impractical because the trucking industry made only 0.5% profit on revenues of 19.3 billion dollars last year. (Source: Business Week, April 18, 1983)
   2. The American Trucking Association is already lobbying heavily against the present weight tax increases from $240 now to $1,600 in July 1984 and $1,900 in July 1988. (Source: Business Week, April 18, 1983)
C. The solution I propose and which is being proposed by the truckers, is an additional tax on diesel fuel just for trucks.
   1. The one disadvantage would be that lighter loaded trucks would be paying for heavier loaded trucks.
   2. Another problem is that the truckers have only proposed a 4 cent hike in the diesel price per gallon. This would probably not be enough to cover the cost of the highway damage. (New Republic 6/13/83)
   3. But, this is the best solution if the tax is increased to 7 cents per gallon; because it has the support of the trucking industry and could probably win passage in Congress and also pay for the needed highway repairs. (Source: New Republic, June 13, 1983)
D. THIS IS A SOLUTION WE CAN OBTAIN AND LIVE WITH TO SOLVE THE SERIOUS PROBLEM OF A DETERIORATING HIGHWAY SYSTEM

ADVANTAGES

IV. This solution will save the average mo-
    torist--like you and me--a great deal of
    money.
    A. It will allow state and local govern-
       ments to pay for needed roads and road
       repairs without raising the average
       motorist taxes.
    B. Instead of paying 110% of the cost we
       will pay our fair share and subsidize
       the trucking industry.
    C. This will also mean that we saved money
       on car repairs because the roads will
       not be torn up and unrepaired--a major
       cause of automotive repair bills.

CONCLUSION—(CLOSURE)

V. What can we--the average citizen—do about
   this solution?
   A. First, we can be aware that the trucks
      are not paying their share of the cost
      of repairing highways they tear up.
   B. Second, we can write our Congressmen
      and Senators in Washington and tell
      them we are tired of paying repair
      bills for the truckers.
   C. Finally, we can ask our Congressmen and
      Senators to support the bill to raise
      the tax on diesel fuel by 7 cents per
      gallon.
   D. Only if all of us voice our outrage and
      concern will we stop paying for things
      that other people are tearing up.

*For effective delivery you can reduce your full-content outline
into a simple phrase outline.*

This full-content outline might be reduced to a phrase outline such
as the following example.

Phrase/Word Outline

```
   I. Trucks signs--$5,500 per year
      --Feel sorry.
      --Remember the rough roads.
  II. Trucks damage highways and don't pay fair
      share for repairs.
      --U.S.D.O.T.--card # 1
      --CBS News--card # 2
      --Gas tax doesn't cover repairs.
      --card # 3
      --Actual cost of damage per lbs.--card # 4
 III. Solutions.
      --Trucks carry ligher loads--uneconomical
      --card # 5
      --Higher road taxes for trucks--imprac-
      tical--card # 6
      --Additional tax on diesel fuel--need a 7
      cent increase
      --card # 7--New Republic source
  IV. Advantages
      --Save average motorist money
      --Allow needed repairs on highways to be
      made.
      --Everyone pays their fair share of
      damage.
   V. Conclusion
      --Be aware trucks are not paying their
      fair share.
      --Write Congress/Senate to pass diesel tax
      increase.
      --Voice your outrage at unfair cost.
```

For information that you are quoting from a source you need to put each piece of information on a note card and number the cards in the order they will appear in the speech.

This word/phrase outline for delivery should reflect the completely planned and developed full-content outline. With practice of the speech even this brief outline will not always be necessary for effective delivery.

Effective speeches are clearly organized and adapted to the specific purpose of the message.

Two Factors That Contribute to the Success of Any Presentation Are

- Clarity and Appropriateness of Organization
- Creation of Audience Interest in the Message

In the following pages we will give you basic organizational patterns (blueprints) that can be applied in the development of various types of speeches.

Shorter Speech Presentations

The Two-Three Minute "Impromptu" Presentation

Many times you will be called on to "say a few words" in a meeting; or, you will be one of several speakers and must make your remarks brief and to the point.

The blueprint for this speech is **P.R.E.P.**

POINT	REASON	EXAMPLE

1. *POINT—Clearly state your point (thesis).* Be brief and clear—make the point a simple declarative statement. This is your stand on an important topic for this audience.

2. *REASON—Why do you want to make this point with this audience? Tell them!!* Tell the audience why this issue should be important to them, at this time.
   Tell them how it affects them and their family, job, or community.

3. *EXAMPLE—Give the audience an example (evidence) to make them believe that the point is true.* Give some specific Factual Example (Who, What, When, How story) that will make the audience believe that your point is probably true.

   Audiences are impressed by the citation of specific facts, statistics, and real situations that prove a problem exists and that it affects them.

4. *RESTATE YOUR POINT—Make sure the audience remembers the point*

The One Point-Speech

This organizational format (blueprint) can be used when you have between five and six minutes for a presentation and your purpose is to convince the audience and persuade them to believe that your point (thesis) is true.

I. *Hook the audience's attention.* Cite a startling fact or Statistic that illustrates the existence of a problem or issue; or, use a humorous story or antidote that can lead into the major point (thesis) you want to make in this speech.

II. *State the point you want to make in this speech.* This should be a simple narrowed declarative statement that is easily understood by the audience.

For Example: *We can get better service for our tax dollar.*

A. *Explain why this point is important to this specific audience.* All audiences want to know why they should be interested in an issue. If they cannot see any relationship between the issue and their lives they will not pay attention and remember what you say.

B. *Prove that the point is true.* Most audiences will demand that you present evidence to prove that your assertions (Thesis statement) are in fact valid. In this portion of the presentation you must present evidence that demonstrates:
   • The problem exists
   • The problem is serious
   • The problem affects this audience
   • Briefly suggest some possible solutions to the problem

C. *Restate your point and conclude the presentation.* Use a Quotation, Story, or Fact that ties this point to the specific point you made in the speech.

Remember: Brevity is a virtue—be specific and to the point, then sit down.

> *Your objective in this type of short speech is to leave the audience with a clear idea of your point and some reason to believe that it is true.*

The Self-Disclosure Speech

This format for a short presentation does not intend to convince or persuade the audience to believe. Instead, the purpose of this type of speech is to inform the audience of a personal belief that affects the speaker. You are asking the audience to understand why you believe something, not necessarily for them to accept or agree with your belief. *You are asking the audience to empathize with you, to see the world from your perspective.*

I. *Hook the audience's attention*. Generally the use of a personal story that illustrates and clarifies your belief is most effective.
II. *State the basic belief (value) that you want to share with the audience*. This should be a simple, brief, easily understood declarative statement. For example: "I believe that hard work is essential for personal fulfillment and success."

A. *Explain how you acquired this belief*. Give the audience several personal examples of things that have happened in your life that made you acquire this basic belief. Here you are revealing a part of your past and asking the audience to see why you believe what you believe.
B. *Explain how this basic belief has affected the way you lead your life and interact with other people*. Give the audience several more examples of situations you have been in where this basic belief has affected the way to respond to situations, events, and other people.
C. *Restate your basic belief and conclude*. Use a quotation, story, or fact that ties this belief to the basic value structure of you and your audience.

The Self-disclosure speech helps to establish a feeling of rapport and empathy between the speaker and the audience. But it is not intended, nor should it be, a purging of our innermost emotions. It is meant to create a bridge of understanding between a speaker and audience.

Short How-to-Do-It Instructional Speech

This speech format is intended to give clear brief instructions on how to perform some rather simple operation. The only purpose of this type of speech is to give the audience information that will help them perform a task.

I. *Hook the audiences' attention*. Tell the audience how this information will be useful to them. If an audience sees no reason for learning how to perform some task—they will not listen or learn.
II. *State the simple operation you are going to explain*. A clear precise sentence.
A. *Explain the process in simple chronological order*. First you do this; Second, you do that, etc., etc., etc.
B. *Remind the audience how this information will be useful to them*.
C. *Ask if there are any questions*.

This format is a brief version of all Informative Speech formats and is useful for most very simple instructional presentations.

Informative Speeches

There are three basic types of Informative Speeches: Lectures, Reports, and Instructional How-to-Do-It presentations.

The two major criteria for Informative Speech effectiveness are:

Clarity of Organization and **Gaining audience interest**

Various organizational patterns can be employed for the organization of the body of the speech such as:

Chronological order; Space Relationships; or, Special Topical arrangement.

The topic will generally determine the type of organizational pattern that you use to develop the body of the speech.

The overall blueprint for any informative speech should follow this simple pattern

I. *Hook the audience interest and attention.*
   - Direct that interest to your topic.
   - Tell the audience why they need this information.
   - Tell the audience why they should listen to you on this topic. Why are you an expert?
II. *State your thesis—the major item of information you intend to cover in the presentation.*
   A. *Summarize in brief precise statements the major divisions of the material you will cover.*
      - Division One
      - Division Two
      - Division Three
      Generally no more than three or four major subpoints or divisions should be developed for clarity and interest.
   B. *Restate Division One.*
      - Explain how this point relates to the total topic.
      - Give examples to clarify the information.
      - Use any other proof material (testimony of fact or opinion, statistics) that will further clarify the material.
      - Restate Division One.
   C. *Restate Division Two.* Follow the same organization as in Division One.
   D. *Restate Division Three.* Follow the same organization as in Division One and Two.

III. *Conclude the speech—restate your major thesis and the major sub-points you covered.*
   A. Remind the audience how they might apply this new information for their benefit.
   B. Tell them where they can get more information on the topic.
   C. Ask if there are any questions.

For an informative speech to be both informative and interesting it must take the audience beyond information they already know and apply that new information to the interest of that specific audience.

Persuasive Speech Formats

The type of Persuasive Speech format utilized depends upon the specific speech purpose and the topic. Generally Persuasive Speeches use either a statement of Fact, Value, or Policy as their Thesis statement. The Four most common and useful formats for persuasive presentations are:

- Problem-Solution Format
- Comparative Advantages Format
- Criteria Format
- Two-Sided Format

Problem-Solution Format

Generally, this format uses a Thesis statement of Policy. For example: "All employees in the transportation industry should be subject to random drug testing." In this statement the speaker is advocating that some course of action, some policy, should be adopted. This format first proves that a problem exist that calls for the solution; then, presents a solution that will solve the problem in a workable, efficient manner; and, finally demonstrates that advantages would occur from the adoption of the solution. Finally it asks for action to get the solution adopted. The example outline at the beginning of this chapter uses this organizational format.

I. *Hook the attention of the audience.* Utilize the techniques that get the audience attention, and direct that attention to the problem.

II. *State the problem that needs to be solved.* For example: "There is a serious, significant drug abuse problem among this nations transportation workers."

   A. *Present the first reason you believe the problem exists.*

      1. Explain the extent and nature of the problem.

      2. Present evidence to establish that the problem really does exist and is serious.

      3. Restate this reason.

   B. *Develop the second and or third reasons you believe the problem exists in the same way you established Reason one.*

III. *State a clear and precise plan that you recommend to solve this problem.*

   A. Demonstrate that your plan (solution) will probably solve the problem.

   B. Demonstrate that your plan (solution) is a practical and workable way to solve the problem.

   C. Answer any possible objections you can think of to the adoption of the plan that your audience might logically raise in their minds.

IV. *Tell the audience what significant advantages they can expect if the solution is adopted.*

V. *Ask the audience to take some action to help get the solution adopted.*

To get an audience to actually take action on your proposal you must convince them that the problems affect them and should be of vital interest to their lives. If the audience does not see that the problems you are talking about affect them they will have little interest in solving those problems.

Comparative-Advantages Format

In the Problem-Solution format you are asserting that there are serious, significant problems that the current policy or programs cannot solve. In using the Comparative-Advantages Format you are comparing the current policy with a proposed new policy to determine which program best achieves the goals/objectives the policy is intended to achieve. You are saying that the new program or policy has significant comparative advantages over the current program or policy if adopted.

I. *Hook the attention of the audience.*
Get the initial attention of your audience and direct that attention to the policy you wish to discuss.

II. *Establish the major goals/objectives that any program in this area should achieve.* These goals/objectives should be logical and appropriate for programs in this area. If possible they should reflect opinions of authorities in the area being discussed.

III. *Present the solution/program that you are proposing to replace the current status-quo program.*

IV. *State the first significant comparative advantage that you claim would occur as a result of adoption of this new program.*
   A. Present evidence that the current program is not achieving this Advantage in the best possible manner.
   B. Present evidence that your proposal would achieve this advantage in a much more efficient manner.

For each comparative advantage you claim for your proposal you need to develop this format—status quo does not achieve the advantage—new program does achieve advantage.

V. *Ask your audience to accept your proposal.* Tell the audience specifically what they can do to help get this new program adopted and ask for their assistance and support.

Criteria Format

While the Problem-Solution and Comparative Advantages formats are usually associated with questions of POLICY, the Criteria Format is utilized with questions of fact or value. When you are asking the audience to make a factual or value judgment without any direct reference to possible solutions or policy considerations you should use this organization blue-print. Some questions of fact and value that are currently being discussed are:

- Is it possible to place men on Mars and Jupiter and safely return them to earth?—A question of Fact.
- Is it probable that the "greenhouse" affect will increase the levels of the oceans and increase the average temperature of the earth?—A question of Fact.
- Is the Japanese Management style best?—A question of Value.
- Is State University a good school?—A question of Value.

To make these factual and value judgments we must first establish valid criteria (standards) that can be used to measure and judge the truth and/or validity of the thesis. Next, we must apply these criteria truth and/or validity of the thesis. Next, we must apply these criteria (standards of judgment) to the available evidence in order to make the judgment of truth/validity.

When establishing the criteria for evaluation it is necessary to make sure that these criteria will be accepted as a proper standard of judgment by your audience. If the audience believes that safety and fuel economy are the major criteria for determining if an automobile is good, you should not establish criteria of styling and speed for making the value judgment.

Unless the criteria established have audience acceptance the thesis (fact/value) will never achieve audience acceptance.

Blue-Print for Criteria Format

I. *Hook the audience's attention.* Get the initial attention of your audience and direct that attention to the Fact or Value you want to discuss.

II. *State your proposition (thesis) of fact or value.*
   A. *Establish the criteria that you will use to evaluate the fact or value.*
      1. First Criteria
      2. Second Criteria
      3. Third Criteria
      These criteria should be logical and agree with authorities in the field and be acceptable as standards of judgement for this audience.
   B. *Restate the first criteria.*
      • Explain and give examples of how this criteria is demonstrated in the item you are discussing.
      • Present solid evidence that the item does in fact conform to and meet this criteria.
      • Restate the Criteria and assert that the item meets this standard of judgement.
   C. *Restate the second, third, fourth criteria and develop each in the same manner as criteria one.*

III. *Restate your thesis of fact or value.*
   A. Remind the audience of how it met each of the criteria.
   B. Ask the audience to believe with you that the Fact or Value is true and valid.

In this type of speech you are merely asking the audience to believe and agree with a judgement of fact or value. You are not asking them to take any specific action based on that belief.

Two-Sided Presentation Format

This format is very similar to the Criteria Format but it adds another element. **Instead of merely establishing the validity of your proposition this format looks at evidence and arguments that might oppose your conclusions then demonstrates that the evidence supporting your thesis is stronger and more valid.**

In many persuasive settings your audience will be exposed to opponents of your point of view. Research has indicated that with an audience that has more than a high school education and are initially neutral or slightly opposed to your point of view a two-sided presentation is more effective than a one-sided presentation in persuading and changing attitudes, and beliefs. Other research has indicated that when an audience that has been exposed to a two-sided presentation is exposed to opposing views they are less likely to accept the second speakers position on issues. But, a word of warning. If your audience has a low level of education the two-sided presentation is more likely to confuse them and they are less likely to accept the speakers position. They seem to become confused when they hear both sides and not know which side to agree with, despite the stronger evidence and logic for the speakers point of view.

Remember

This format should be used only with

- Audiences that have a higher level of education.
- Audiences that are neutral or slightly opposed to your point.
- Audiences that are likely to hear opposing points of view.

Two-Sided Presentation Blueprint

I. *Hook the attention of your audience.* Get the initial attention of your audience and direct it to the topic.
II. *State the topic in a neutral manner.* For example: Is the Japanese or American car the better product?
   It is best to state your thesis as a question so that when you present the two sides you are attempting to answer that question by looking at both sides of the evidence.
   A. *Establish the various issues/arguments concerning the topic you are going to consider.* Here you are previewing the audience with the major arguments and issues.
   B. Restate the question.

III. *State your first major issue.*
   A. Explain and give a brief summary of the evidence opposing your point of view.
   B. Explain and give a longer summary of the evidence that supports your point of view.
   C. Point out how the evidence supporting your point of view is more valid than the evidence on the opposing side.
IV. *State your second, third, and fourth issues and develop them in the same manner as issue one (above).*
 V. *Conclude your speech by asking your audience to believe that your side of the argument should prevail and that at some future date they should act upon that belief.*

Before you use this organizational format you should honestly believe that the weight of evidence and argument on the issues you consider do in fact support your point of view.

The advantage you have with this format is that the audience will feel that they have objectively considered both sides of the relevant issues and arguments and have come to a conclusion based on their judgement of the evidence. The speaker will appear to merely be giving relevant information to the audience so they can make this "objective" judgement.

Remember

- Organizational clarity is important for audience acceptance and belief of your ideas.
- You should develop a clear, detailed outline (blue print) of your ideas.
- You should use the organizational format that best fits your speech purpose.
- Organizational clarity and getting and keeping audience interest and attention are vital to communication success.

CHAPTER 7

Listening

We Spend a Great Deal of Our Communication Time in Listening

Studies show that we spend seven out of every ten minutes that we are alive and awake communicating verbally. Our time is devoted 9% to writing, 16% to reading, 30% to speaking, and **45% to listening.** Although we spend more time in listening than any communication activity, we receive the least training in improving our listening skills. The following suggestions should help you become a more effective listener.

Listening Quiz

Answer the following statements "yes" or "no".

- _____ 1. Hearing and listening are the same.
- _____ 2. Listening is automatic and cannot be taught.
- _____ 3. Speaking is more important than listening in the communication process.
- _____ 4. I often stop listening after a few sentences if I think the message is uninteresting.
- _____ 5. I judge the speaker's voice, gestures, clothes and hair style.
- _____ 6. I try to outline all speeches while listening.
- _____ 7. I often daydream while trying to listen.
- _____ 8. I immediately try to think of questions and comments to dispute the evidence if I disagree with the speaker's message.
- _____ 9. I stop listening if the message is too difficult to understand.
- _____ 10. I stop listening if I have already heard the information.
- _____ 11. I listen for the facts in the message.
- _____ 12. My attention is easily distracted by noise or movement.

If you answered yes to any of the above statements, you have some misconceptions about listening (statements 1–3) or **Poor Listening habits** (statements 4–12).

Listening Is a Responsibility of Effective Communication

Most people believe effective communication is the sole responsibility of the speaker. **This is not true.** The responsibility must be equally shared by the speaker and listener.
Not listening stops communication as quickly as not speaking.

Hearing versus Listening—There Is a Difference

Hearing is the automatic physiological process of RECEIVING SOUNDS through the sensory channel.

Listening is the voluntary mental process of ASSIGNING MEANING AND RESPONDING to the sights and sounds.

Listening requires attention, patience, concentration, interpretation and sometimes evaluation.

The Purpose for Listening Is Important to Effective Listening

As listeners we must determine the main purpose of each listening situation. In order to accomplish this goal we must be able to recognize the different types of listening situations.

Listening for Enjoyment/Appreciation. As we listen for enjoyment we are usually concerned with something other than just a message. We listen for the *sensory pleasures of presentation.* Some examples are concerts, plays and movies.

Listening for Information. When we listen for information we should *understand the message* thus increasing our knowledge. Some examples are news programs, lectures and reports.

Listening to Evaluate. As we listen to evaluate we must not only *comprehend* the message, we should recognize the facts, separate those facts from emotional appeals, *determine the soundness* of the *logic and evidence and assign some worth* to the content. Some examples are commercials, political campaigns and persuasive speeches.

Listening to Support. As we listen to support we are acting as a "sounding board", *giving another person an opportunity to share ideas and feelings* or talk through a problem and the solutions. As a supportive listener we must be totally aware of another's mood and feelings. Some examples are professional therapy sessions and informal encounters with friends.

Ten Guides to More Effective Listening[1]

1. Find Areas of Interest. All studies point to the advantage in being interested in the topic under discussion. Poor listeners usually declare the subject uninteresting after a few sentences. Once this decision is made, it serves to rationalize any and all inattention to the message.

Good listeners follow different tactics. They realize the key to the whole matter of interest in a topic is the word use. Whenever we wish to listen efficiently, we ought to say to ourselves: "What is the speaker saying that I can use? What worthwhile ideas are they presenting? Are they reporting any workable procedures? Anything that I can cash in on, or with which I can make myself happier?" Such questions lead us to screen what we are hearing in a continual effort to sort out the elements of personal value.

2. Judge Content, Not Delivery. Many listeners alibi inattention to a speaker by thinking to themselves: "Who could listen to such a character? What an awful voice! Will he ever stop reading from those notes?"

The good listener reacts differently. They may look at the speaker and think, "This person is inept, a nerd. Seems like almost anyone could talk better than that." But from this initial similarity he moves on to a different conclusion, thinking, "But wait a minute . . . I'm not interested in personality or delivery. I want to find out what the speaker knows. *Does this speaker know things that I need to know?*"

1. Nichols, Ralph. *The Speech Teacher,* Vol. X, No. 2, (March 1961, p. 118) Reprinted by permission of the author.

3. Hold Your Fire. Overstimulation is almost as bad as understimulation, and together constitute the twin evils of inefficient listening. The overstimulated listeners get too excited, or excited too soon, by the speaker. Also the listener desires to enter immediately into the argument and beomes preoccupied with this goal while subsequent passages of the speakers message go unheard.

We must learn not to get too excited about a speaker's point until we are certain we thoroughly understand it. We must always withhold evaluation until our comprehension is complete.

4. Listening for Ideas. Good listeners focus on central ideas; they tend to recognize the characteristic language in which central ideas are usually stated, and they are able to discriminate between fact and principle, idea and example, evidence and argument. Poor listeners are inclined to listen for the facts in every presentation and not comprehend the ideas the facts are meant to support.

5. Be Flexible. Poor listeners believe there is only one way to take notes—by making an outline. Unfortunately not all formal speeches are carefully organized. There are few things more frustrating than trying to outline an unorganized presentation.

Good listeners have more than one system of taking notes and adjust their system to the organizational pattern, or the absence of one in each situation. If we want to be good listeners, we must be flexible and adaptable note-takers.

6. Work at Listening. Poor listeners do not spend any energy in a listening situation. The overrelaxed listener is merely appearing to tune in, and then feeling conscience-free to pursue mental tangents.

Good listeners work hard. For selfish reasons alone one of the best investments we can make is to give each speaker our conscious attention. We should establish eye contact; indicate by posture and facial expression that the occasion and the speaker's efforts are a matter of real concern to us. When we do these things we help the speaker to express himself more clearly, and we in turn profit by better understanding of the improved communication we have helped to achieve.

7. Resist Distractions. Good listeners tend to adjust quickly to any kind of abnormal situation. Poor listeners tend to be readily influenced by distractions and, in some instances, create distractions themselves.

8. Exercise Your Mind.   Poor listeners are inexperienced in listening to any difficult, technical or expository material. . . . Good listeners develop an appetite for listening to a variety of presentations difficult enough to challenge their mental capacities. Inexperience is not quickly solved. Knowledge of our weakness may help us. *We need never become too old to meet new challenges.*

9. Keep Your Mind Open.   Parallel to the blind spots are certain psychological deaf spots which impair our ability to perceive and understand. These deaf spots are the dwelling place of our most cherished notions, convictions and complexes. Often, when a speaker invades one of these areas with a word or phrase, we turn our mind to retraveling familiar mental pathways criss-crossing our invaded area of sensitivity.

Effective listeners try to identify and rationalize the words or phrases most upsetting emotionally. Often the emotional impact of such words can be decreased through a free and open discussion with friends.

10. Capitalize on Thought Speed.   Most persons talk at a speed of about 125 words a minute. There is good evidence that if thought were measured in words per minute most of us could think easily at about four times that rate. Thus we normally have about 400 words of thinking time to spare during every minute a person talks to us.

What do we do with our excess thinking time? Poor listeners become impatient and start thinking about something else for a moment, then dart back to the speaker. These brief side excursions continue until our mind stays too long on some irrelevant subject. When we return to the speaker, we find they are far ahead of us. Now it's more difficult to follow the speaker and much easier to take off on more mental side excursions. Finally we give up, the speaker is still talking; but, our mind is in another world.

The good listener uses this thought speed to his/her advantage; constantly applying the spare thinking time to what is being said. This is not difficult once we have a definite pattern to follow. To develop such a pattern we should:

Try to Anticipate What a Person Is Going to Talk About.   On the basis of what has been said, ask yourself, "What is the speaker trying to get at? What point is the speaker going to make?"

Mentally Summarize What the Speaker Has Been Saying.   What point has been made already?

Weigh the Speaker's Evidence by Mentally Questioning It. Are the facts, examples and statistics correct? Do they come from a credible and non-bias source? Am I getting the full picture from this speaker?

Listen Between the Lines. The speaker doesn't always put everything that's important into words. Remember non-verbal ques—the changing vocal tones and volume, the tilt of the head, the raising of the eyebrow—may have meaning.

Not capitalizing on thought speed is our greatest single handicap. The difference between thought speed and speech speed breeds mental tangents. Yet through listening training, this difference can be converted into an asset.

Remember

- Effective communication requires effective listening.
- Effective listening requires active participation.
- Active participation requires attention, patience and concentration.
- Effective listeners understand better, remember longer and form closer bonds with other people.

CHAPTER 8

Small Group Participation and Leadership

Group discussion is a cooperative process involving three or more individuals verbally interacting face-to-face exchanging and evaluating ideas, and information in order to learn more about a subject or solve a problem of mutual concern.

Group Types and Purposes

Learning Group: The purpose of a learning group is to share information in order to gain understanding of a subject. Learning groups are often used in the classroom and at professional conventions.

Decision-Making Problem Solving Group: The purpose of the decision-making or problem solving group is to exchange and evaluate ideas and information in order to arrive at an agreement concerning a future policy or course of action. A committee is an example of this type of group.

Buzz Group: The purpose of the buzz group is to involve all members of an audience in the discussion. The large group is divided into smaller groups of 4–6 individuals including a chairperson. Each group discusses one aspect of the topic or problem. Following the discussion, the chairperson presents the opinions of the group to the entire audience.

Brainstorming Group: The purpose of brainstorming is to create a quantity of ideas in a short amount of time. During a brainstorming session, evaluation and criticism are forbidden while contributions and originality are encouraged. The primary goal is quantity of ideas not quality. Brainstorming is often used in problem-solving group when the group is discovering possible solutions to the problem.

Panel: The purpose of the panel is to exchange ideas and information before an audience in order to present information or solve a problem. The panel usually consists of 4–6 members and a chairperson. Panel members do not have prepared speeches but have knowledge concerning the topic and a carefully planned discussion outline or agenda. The chairperson provides introductory remarks, summaries and transitions, BUT, does not contribute ideas and information during the discussion. After the discussion, the audience is allowed to question individual panel members.

Group Characteristics

Norms   Norms are guidelines for acceptable group-behavior that are established or perceived to be established by most group members. Norms develop identifiable patterns for completing tasks and communicating with one another thus providing order and structure to the discussion.

Cohesiveness   Cohesiveness is the common bond among group members. The members are attracted to each other because of similar values, needs and interests. Also, they receive satisfaction from interacting with one another and share a commitment to the groups activities and goals.

Conflict   Conflict is disagreement among group members. Conflict is considered constructive when it forces the group members to critically examine the ideas and information in order to reach a decision. Some conflict is essential for a productive discussion but it should not become bitter or emotionalized. Interpersonal conflict is destructive because it changes the focus of the discussion for the issues to the personalities of group members.

Status and Power   Status is the perceived importance of individual members of the group. Power is the ability to influence other members. Group members can increase their power or status by performing in certain ways to gain approval by other group members. Power and status affects the ways in which group members communicate and should be used to influence others to accomplish group goals not as a means to manipulate behavior.

Group Functions

Task Functions   Task functions fulfill the structure and content needs of the group. Task functions include contributing ideas and information, asking questions, clarifying ideas, recording information and making procedural comments thus moving the discussion toward the accomplishment of the groups' goals.

Maintenance Functions   Maintenance functions fulfill the interpersonal needs of the group. Preserving the group as a social unit builds positive relationships thus making it possible for the group member to work together and feel good about their accomplishments.

Role Behavior in Groups During a group discussion each member may play various roles in order to fulfill task and maintenance roles. Some individual roles are negative and cause serious problems for group interaction and productivity.

Methods to Achieve Group Task Goals

1. Contribute accurate information and opinions that are based on accurate information.
2. Ask questions concerning facts and opinions that others present. Listen with an open mind and ask for clarification and explanation of points you do not understand.
3. Draw inferences and conclusions based on information that you and others present.
4. Summarize what the group has already accomplished and what the group still needs to accomplish.
5. Encourage participation by all members of the group.
6. Raise questions as to the validity of information, opinions and conclusions presented. Don't be afraid to challenge the consensus of the group if you think it is not logical or supported by evidence.
7. Record the groups progress so that at the conclusion of the discussion the group will have a record of its proceedings.

Methods to Achieve Group Interpersonal Cohesiveness

1. Make members of the group feel positive toward their contributions and their position in the group.
2. Mediate conflicts of ideas and/or personalities within the group so that personal differences do not prevent the group from achieving its' task.
3. Keep the group directed toward the accomplishment of its' task goals.
4. Keep the group aware of the standards and requirements of the task goals.

Negative Tactics to Avoid

For a group to be successful it has to keep the task clearly defined; keep good interpersonal relationships; and, avoid negative tactics that disrupt either task or interpersonal success within the group.

1. Don't make personal attacks on other members of the group.
2. Don't object to ideas and proposals just to be objecting. If you object to something you should have a logical reason based on solid evidence of reasonable assumptions.
3. Don't draw attention to your own personal success or problems that have no relevance to the group task.
4. Don't talk merely to gain attention whether or not you have a contribution to make to the task or interpersonal success of the group.
5. Don't plead your own special interest if it is not in the best interest of the accomplishment of the groups task goals.

Leadership

Leadership is the degree to which a person directs and regulates group interaction and decision making. There are three basic leadership styles:

Authoritarian: An authoritarian leader dictates policy, makes all major decisions and feels the task achievement is much more important than the people involved.

Democratic: The democratic leader distributes power among group members balancing the task and maintenance functions.

Laissez-Faire: A laissez-faire leader allows group members to proceed with very little guidance or control.

The most effective style is determined by the nature of the group task, relationships between the leader and group members, and the amount of control the group needs to accomplish goals.

Effective Problem-Solving Discussion

Preparing for a successful discussion requires the same methods that you would employ in planning for the delivery of a successful Problem-Solving Speech (See discussion of Problem-Solving Speech purpose and format in Chapter Six).

Preparation: In preparing for a problem-solving discussion the group members must determine the objectives, select a discussion format, formulate the discussion questions and obtain relevant information concerning those questions.

Objectives: The group's objectives must be defined and accepted by group members.

Format: The group needs step-by-step guidance provided by a problem-solving format.

I. *Recognize and Define the Problem.*
  • How does it affect the immediate interest and purpose of this group?
  • What is the groups purpose in considering this problem?

II. *Determine the Extent, Seriousness and Impact of the Problem.*
  What are the indications that this problem exists?
  What are the causes of this problem?
  How serious are these indications of a problem to:
  • Society in general
  • The constitution of this group
  • The individual members of the group
  What is the IMPACT-SIGNIFICANCE of this problem(s)?

III. *What **criteria** must be met by any solution that the group might adopt to solve the problem?*
  • What problems must be solved for a successful solution?
  • What laws, customs, beliefs, standards must be preserved by any successful solution?
  • What is the minimum level acceptable in any solution?
  • What is the ideal (maximum) level for the solution of the problem?

IV. *What are the **possible solutions?***
  • What is the cost—both financial and human?
  • Is the solution practical?
  • Is the solution workable?
  • **Will the solution solve the problem?**
  • Of all possible solutions suggested which one or ones best solve the total problem?
  • Does this solution meet the Criteria established?

V. *How can this group implement this solution?*
  • What specific actions must the group and group members take to implement the solution?
  • What is the probable time table for implementation of the solution?
  • Who is responsible for specific actions for implementation?
  • How will the group keep track of the process of implementation?

The Use of Questions of Fact, Value, Policy Are the Building Blocks for Successful Problem-Solving Discussions

This Problem-Solving Discussion format provides the organizational pattern but the group members must provide relevant questions and information for each level of the format. Questions can be worded as fact, value or policy depending on the type of information the group needs in order to accomplish objectives.

Questions of Fact: "Is it true or not true?"

Questions of Value: "Is it good or bad?" These require assessment of the worth of some object, situation, or idea. Questions of fact should be answered before considering a question of value.

Questions of Policy: These ask what should be done. Questions of fact and value should be answered before choosing a course of action.

Research: Group members must locate and evaluate information relevant to the discussion topic. Information can be obtained from various library sources, conducting surveys, and interviewing experts.

Successful group discussion for problem solving must rest on the discovery of relevant evidence of fact and value that prove the nature and extent of a problem and the workability, practicality, and solvency of the solutions.

Forming the Small Discussion Group

Size: The group must be large enough to provide needed ideas and information but small enough to insure participation for all members.

Order: Order can be maintained if members are courteous to each other and keep their contributions relevant.

Willingness to Compromise: The group's purpose must take priority over the individual member's goals.

Feeling of Accomplishment: The group must set a goal that is understood by all members and work together toward the attainment.

Leader's Qualities

Effective Communication: The leader should have the capacity for rapid analysis and be able to express ideas clearly. (See the suggested positive actions that group members must take for successful group task and interpersonal goals listed in this chapter).

Group Commitment: The leader should remain impartial and be committed to the group goals and needs encouraging members to contribute their ideas and information. Also, the leader should have the skills to insure the fulfillment of maintenance as well as task functions.

Leader's Duties:
1. Get the discussion started.
2. Follow the discussion format.
3. Encourage members to contribute ideas and information.
4. Insure participation by all members of the group.
5. Help resolve conflict.
6. Provide summaries.

Participant's Qualities

Effective Communicator: The participant should be an effective listener as well as an effective speaker and be willing to listen and learn from others. (See the suggested positive actions that group members must take in a discussion listed earlier in this chapter).

Knowledge of the Subject Under Discussion: The participant should have information concerning all aspects of the topic under discussion.

Participant's Duties:
1. Listen to other members ideas and information.
2. Contribute new ideas and information.
3. Speak if you can clarify a point made by another member.
4. Ask and answer questions.
5. Contribute when you can correct an error.
5. Speak if you can make an intelligent comment or suggestion.

Remember
- Effective group discussion requires leaders and participants that understand the discussion process.
- Effective group discussion requires the understanding and utilization of task and maintenance functions.

CHAPTER 9

Interviewing

You are called into your boss's office for a yearly evaluation. She proceeds to ask you a series of questions about your feelings toward your present position. You in turn question her on how she feels you have been performing and receive positive feedback. She concludes the meeting by handing you a copy of her written evaluation of your performance in the job, and urges you to contact her if you have any questions. She continues her work, and you get up and leave.

While walking down the street a person approaches you carrying a clipboard and asks if you would mind participating in a survey. You have no objection to participating and proceed to answer a series of yes/no and multiple choice questions. After a few minutes you proceed on your way.

You go in to purchase a new car and a salesman helps you. He follows you around asking questions as to the type of car and the price range you are interested in purchasing. After showing you several cars you ask the salesman questions concerning each of the cars and the financing available. You leave with a brand new automobile and the salesman proceeds to another customer.

All of these situations have several things in common. Two parties interacting, asking and responding to questions, receiving immediate nonverbal and verbal feedback, with an expressed purpose behind the meeting. *These encounters are all different types of interviews.*

An interview is communication between two parties usually involving the asking and answering of questions with a serious predetermined goal or objective.

Public Speaking vs. Interviews

In public speaking you are usually addressing your message to a large group of people. The amount of feedback you receive from your audience is at times minimal to none. The amount of analysis you engage in only allows you to describe your audience in general terms. You have very little chance to determine how effectively your message is being received by every member of the audience.

Interviews Have Many Advantages Over Public Speaking. The immediacy of the feedback, the ability to analyze your audience much better, and the flexibility of being able to switch roles from sender to receiver throughout the interview. These factors give you a significant advantage in making sure your message is understood. A well conducted interview can communicate more information more effectively than almost any other form of communication.

Many of the Skills Which Are Involved in Public Speaking Are Also Involved in Interviewing. It is important in interviewing to be able to organize your thoughts, to do a thorough analysis of your audience and to present yourself in such a way as to gain credibility with your audience. The major difference between public speaking and interviewing is that you will be the source and the audience of messages in this setting. *In interviewing there are two parties participating in sending and receiving messages.*

You may consider yourself the interviewer (R) but, at times during the interview you may find yourself the interviewee (E). In interviews it is usually the responsibility of both parties to be the audience and the speaker at different times.

Most of us have developed our interviewing skills from watching other interviews and from helpful tips provided by our friends and professional associates. It is important to consider that interviewing is a skill and that practicing bad habits over and over again will not make you a better interviewer. It is similar to a basketball player that practices hitting the backboard because he noticed that all good basketball players know how to hit the backboard. He is practicing from a bad model. This chapter will attempt to introduce you to correct interviewing skills.

Planning for the Interview

An interview is goal oriented. This is the major difference that separates an interview from casual conversation. Two friends getting together for lunch and discussing various topics that happen to cross their minds are not in an interviewing situation, there is no goal to their discussion. Two people meeting to discuss potential employment over lunch is an interviewing situation. There is a definite goal to their discussion. It is important when entering an interviewing situation to **recognize and define the goals of the interview.**

Pre-planning

When planning an interview you should consider four factors: 1) **The goals of the interview,** 2) **the situation in which the interview will take place,** 3) **the background of the participants in the interview and their points of view, and** 4) **the role you will play in the interview.** All of these factors are interrelated. The goal of the interview affects the situation in which the interview will occur and these factors combined with your knowledge of the other person in the interview will give a good indication a to the role you should play in the interview.

For example you get a lead from an old friend and go to an employment interview at his company.

1. Recognize the Goals of the Interview. There are usually two sets of goals in any interview. Each party brings their own goals and attitudes to the interview. It is your job as an active participant to realize the other persons goals and to achieve common goals.

Example: You are entering an employment interview with the goals of presenting yourself as best you can and to obtain the position you are seeking. It is the goal of the interviewer to find the best person for the position that she can. It is important for you to impress the interviewer (R) that you are the best person for that position. The more you can make your goals overlap the more likely you are to achieve your own goals.

2. Acknowledge the Situation in Which the Interview Occurs. It is important for you to take into account all the situational variables that will enter into the interview. No interview occurs in a void. Each interview you will have will be affected by the situation in which it occurs. You must accept these factors and use them to your advantage if possible.

3. Research the Background of the Other Person in the Interview. As in a public speaking situation it is important to know the background of your audience. You would feel foolish arriving at an NRA banquet expecting to give a speech advocating handgun control legislation. Just as you would feel foolish trying to sell a Toyota to the CEO of General Motors. It is imperative that you know the background of the participants and their role as it applies to the goal of this interview.

4. Realize the Role You Will Be Playing in the Interview. As in any social situation you are expected to conform to certain social standards. The same is true in interviews. The term "role" describes the image that you wish to present to the other person. If you are applying for a managerial position at Proctor & Gamble, you would want to present an image consistent with what the interviewer expects from a manager at Proctor & Gamble. This is true with all interviews. You should take all factors into account and react as best you can to the role relationships and situational demands.

Interviews Are Structured Around Questions

Questions are the building blocks of a good interview. It is the questions and the answers that make an interview such an effective means of communication. The better phrased the questions and answers, the better the interview.

Open vs. Closed Questions

Open questions are questions which allow the interviewee to take control of the interview for a while. It is a way of getting large amounts of unspecific information. For example: "Tell me about your education?" Or, "What is your greatest strength as a person?"

Closed questions on the other hand are very specific and leave the interviewee with very few options for response. The purpose of closed questions is to solicit precise bits of information. For example: "How old are you?" Or, "Where did you work last?"

Bi-Polar Questions

Bi-polar questions are closed questions with only two options: yes or no, true or false. For example: "Do you like precision work?" Or, "Do you have a drivers' license?"

Primary and Secondary Questions

Primary questions are used to introduce new topics into an interview. Secondary or "follow-up" questions follow-up the topic area introduced by the primary questions. Secondary questions allow an interviewer to probe for more information or to clarify an answer. For example when the area of educational experience has been introduced by primary questions, follow up questions might probe as to strengths and weakness in that preparation.

Interview Structure

The structure of an interview is very similar to the structure of a public speech or a well written essay. It should have a beginning—**opening,** a middle—**body,** and an end—**closing.** As in a public speech you must introduce the topics to be discussed in a logical coherent order that furthers the achieving of the goal of the interview. You must discuss those topics in the predetermined order and conclude the discussion.

Opening

The opening of the interview should have a three-fold function:

1. It should allow the participants in the interview to introduce and acquaint themselves with one another.
2. It should acquaint the interviewee (E) with the purpose of the interview.
3. It should present the topics to be discussed in the interview.

Examples of an Opening:

R: Hello my name is John Smith, I work for Ford in Customer Relations and I am calling to inquire about your new Mercury Tracer. I have a short list of questions, I would like to ask about your new car. You are John Q. Public, correct?

E: Yes.

Body

The body of the interview should cover the major topic areas necessary to achieve the goal of the interview. In this portion of the interview the Interviewer (R) can be either directive or non-directive in their approach. This simply refers to the amount of control that the interviewer chooses to take on the directon of the interview. A highly directive interview is one in which the Interviewer (R) completely controls the progress of the interview by extensive use of bipolar or multiple choice questions. The Interviewee (E) has little or no chance to change the direction or progress of the interview. A survey or poll is a good example of a highly directive interview. Such interviews are usually highly scheduled (planned) and extremely standardized. This allows for computer coding of results. Non-directive interviews have less rigid schedules (plans of questions) and allow for more primary open-ended questions followed by secondary probing questions. The non-directive interview requires an Interviewer with more experience and skill than the directive interview. The non-directive interview is best for problem-solving, evaluation, and job interviewing.

Closing

The interview is not completed until a final determination on the purpose and goal of the interview has been reached by both parties. It is important that the closing of the interview not be taken lightly. This is the last impression that both the Interviewer (R) and the Interviewee (E) will leave. A poor closing can defeat the entire goal of the interview.

Types of Interview Settings and Suggested Organizational Patterns (Schedules)

Survey Interview

1. Select Topic Areas.   Select the topics to be covered in the interview. Determine what information you want out of each topic area.

2. Determine the Structuring of the Topics.   Decide what information to ask for first and what to ask for last. It is important to consider that in most surveys the Interviewee (E) can end the interview at any point. So starting out a survey with extremely personal questions will cause many people to immediately terminate the interview.

3. Determine the Questions to Be Used.   It is important in a survey to phrase all the questions completely and clearly. The questions are to be read to Interviewees and Interviewers will fill in their short answers on the same survey sheet. **Therefore, it is of extreme importance that all questions are clear, brief and straight forward.**

4. Determine Population to Be Sampled and Sample Size.   You must decide how many people should be included in this survey. A well run survey can allow people to generalize to the entire population they wish to investigate. But this is extremely expensive and time consuming. The Gallup poll is an excellent example of a very accurate measure of U.S. public opinion. To conduct such an accurate survey for total population generalization is difficult and expensive. Most survey interviews are simply used to indicate probable problem areas and suggest probable acceptable solutions for those problem areas.

5. Pretest the Survey.   It is important that the survey be pretested so most problems with the survey questions can be identified and corrected in advance of mass interviewing.

6. Conduct the Survey (Interviews).   An adequate number of surveys should be run to get a good cross section of responses and differing possibilities. You should be sure that the population you are interested in are the populations that are responding to the survey.

7. Tabulating Results.   Most survey interviews should be structured so that they can be tabulated and analyzed by the use of computers. You should be able to code the type of respondent and the responses of those individual types of respondent.

For a more detailed explanation of this type of interview it is recommended that you consult text that deal specifically with survey research and interviewing.

Employee Evaluation Interview

1. Research Information on Employee Performance. If there have been previous evaluations then these should be read and considered. If there are any reports concerning the employee and their performance on specific job assignments those should be considered. All information concerning the employee's performance should be researched. *Be sure to have an exact job description for the employee's position and be sure that the employee was aware of this job description when hired.*

2. Select Job Performance Areas to Be Reviewed. On the basis of your research select the areas of Job performance that should be discussed with the employee. These areas should include positive aspects of the job performance as well as the problem areas that your research has discovered.

3. State Specific Job Performance Criteria. It is important that the Interviewer (Manager) (R) and the Interviewee (Employee) (E) have a clear understanding of the criteria that are relevant in the evaluation of performance. The Interviewer should have a clear list, but also allow the employee to suggest other criteria that might be relevant to the job performance evaluation.

4. Apply the Criteria for the Job to the Employee Performance. This is the basis of the Body of this type of interview. Each criteria should be considered, one at a time, and discussed. It is important that the discussion be confined to job-related activities and performance and that emotional personality factors be suppressed in this discussion.

5. Make Positive Suggestions of Specific Improvements. Both the Interviewer and Interviewee should contribute to suggestions for positive improvement in job performance. An employee that has the opportunity to present their side of performance situations and helps to come to conclusions for improvements will be more likely to actually improve in their job performance.

6. Provide the Employee with a Written Evaluation Form. This form should be signed by the Evaluator and by the Employee being evaluated so that it is clear that the criteria or evaluation and the recommendations for improvement are clearly understood by both parties.

Problem-Solution Interview

The format for this type of interview is very similar to the format for a Problem-Solution speech or group discussion. You might review the sections on these two types of communication settings in previous chapters of this book.

1. Analyze the Extent and Nature of the Problem. Before you can ask another person to help you solve a problem you must first do extensive research so you know the facts and evidence that prove a problem exist. You should ask: What is the extent of the problem? How serious and significant is the problem, to me and to the person I am asking for help? What is the impact of the problem on me, and on the other person?

2. Develop a List of Problem Areas That Affect Both You and the Person You Are Interviewing. Remember until the Interviewee (E) is convinced that the problem affects them, they will see little or no reason to help you in solving that problem. If you are losing business that is only your problem, unless you can convince the Interviewee that your loss of business affects them in some significant manner.

3. Develop Suggestions for Solutions of the Problems. Remember that the solutions to the problems must be acceptable to both the Interviewer (R) and to the Interviewee (E). You should determine what the ideal solution might be for both parties and also what the minimum acceptable solution would be from your point of view.

4. Develop Methods of Implementation for the Adoption of Possible Solutions. A solution is effective only when it is put into operation. In this step you should consider who will be responsible for which aspects of the solution; what timetable must be followed to implement the solution; what future communications must be used to check on the progress of the solution.

5. Set a Time for Any Follow-Up Interview That Might Be Needed to Implement the Solution.

Employment Interview

1. Research the Company You Are Interviewing. Compile all information concerning the company you will be interviewing with. This will aid you in determining whether you would enjoy working for the company and helps in developing questions for you to ask in the interview.

2. Research the Position You Are Applying for. Know what the expectations and responsibilities are for the position. Determine what abilities, talents, and training makes you the best person for this position. Determine any weakness you may have in preparation or training and decide how to compensate for those areas in presenting your qualifications.

3. Prepare for Possible Questions That the Interviewer Might Ask and Prepare Questions You Want Answered by the Interviewer Concerning the Job Position. Most placement services have a list of the twenty to thirty most commonly asked questions in a job interview. Obtain such a list and be prepared for those questions. Generally they concern your preparation, your job background, your career ambitions and expectations, your ability to solve problems, and your general character. You should prepare questions that you want answered concerning the duties, responsibilities, advancement opportunities, advanced educational opportunities, and other conditions concerning this position. It is a good idea to take an extra resume and a copy of all your references. If a transcript was requested be sure you have one available.

4. Take Notes During the Interview So You Will Be Sure to Remember Important Points.

5. Find Out What the Expected Time Frame is on Filling the Position.

6. Write a Follow-Up Letter. It may help to follow your interview with a letter of thanks to your interviewer. It puts your name in front of them one more time. In hopes that they will remember you when the person is selected for the job.

Remember

- Interviews involve both people speaking and listening.
- Interviews utilize questions and answers to convey messages and responses that move the interview toward its goal.
- Interviews should always have a clear goal or purpose.
- Interviews should have a clear organizational structure (schedule) to achieve this goal.

CHAPTER 10

Organizational Communication

Organizational communication is the study of how organizations communicate both internally and externally. **Organizational communication is human communication in an organizational setting.** We are all involved in several different organizations, whether as a student, employee, elected representative or just as a citizen. You are surrounded by and participating in many organizations.

You are involved when you receive a memo on a new company policy (formal internal communication channel) when your friend from another department tells you about a personnel change in his department and how other departments are being affected (informal internal communication channel); when you work at a summer job where the manager treats all employees as if they are lazy, inefficient, and working only for their paychecks (Theory X Management). **Organizational communications strategies affect every moment of our working lives.**

Organizational communication applies terms and models to describe actual situations in the hopes of being able to better understand how organizations work and how they can work more effectively. If an organization does not recognize how their employees receive and process information they cannot evaulate their communication effectiveness and methods to improve that effectiveness. It is necessary to recognize problems before effective solutions can be considered and implemented.

This chapter will introduce you briefly to some of the theories and terms involved in Organizational Communication.

Organizational Theories

Classical Theory

Most "classical" theories view the organization as a machine. Each person (worker) is a part of this machine. The machine runs well as long as all the parts work efficiently together. This is still a rather popular view of American business and industry. This theory believes that if one piece of the machine breaks down a new part can be put into place and the organization will continue without disruption. This theory believes that it is more important that the organization survives than that the individual person within the organization survives.

These ideas have their **advantages.** It is important to realize for an organization to thrive and continue it is imperative that hierarchies and rules be established. For an organization to continue it must be able to live without anyone special person or persons. For example, the Catholic Church was founded on the teachings and person of Jesus Christ and

Jesus's relationship to Peter. From this all of the present Catholic church has arisen. None of this would have been possible without the strict organizational rules and hierarchies established by the early church.

There are also **serious drawbacks** to considering an organization as a machine. The idea that everyone is replaceable and that the best way to run an organization is to press employees to fit the position in which they are placed leaves out the human side of any organization. The organization must ask, "Is it more important to the company for an employee to perform as a cog in a large machine; or, is it more important that the employee's individual abilities and freedom be considered to allow for an altering of their job description to better suit those individual talents.

Henry Ford implemented one of the first assembly line production facilities. The Ford Motor Company was based on the worker as a cog in an assembly line theory. If the worker did not do their part the entire machine would break down. Yet, recently Ford has begun to consider quality circles where workers give input as to how the cars are built.

An organization made up of people can never be accurately represented as a well oiled machine.

Human Relations Theory

Human Relations theory is based on the idea that to get the most out of workers they should be satisfied in their job. A happy worker is a productive worker. This means that the organization should be viewed through the eyes of the man on the assembly line or the data entry clerk in front of the computer screen. This theory asks: "How does the organization benefit John Q. Worker? What are his concerns and needs?"

An example of this theory in operation is very simple. John is displeased with his job. He is forced to go out every day and meet with clients to try and sell electronic parts. John is the client representative for the company. He is paid a good salary but he is not happy with his job. He joined X Electronics because he wanted to become a project engineer and design electronic devices. But the company policy says that first an entry level employee must be a client representative before they may move anywhere else in the organization. John will quit unless the company moves him to Research & Development. The question confronting the company is the benefit of keeping John, who has an M.S. in Electrical Engineering, versus losing him and maintaining a rigid company policy. *Are rules made to maintain a status-quo, or are they made to facilitate the achievement of productivity/profit goals of an organization?*

There are **disadvantages** in the Human Relations perspective. It is important to remember that not all happy workers are productive, in fact some workers may be happiest doing nothing. If a company considers only how the worker is affected, then the overall organizational picture may be sacrificed and productivity and profit lost. An organization must also consider the outside environments affect on the entire organization.

Systems Theory

Systems theory is based on the concept that organizations are complex systems interrelated to other complex systems. This theory emphasizes that you should view an organization as being an organism made up of interconnected and interdependent organs. This view allows you to see the organization as being a part of the larger society with outside forces affecting the inner workings. *This model of organizations attempts to put the organization in an overall framework.*

The **advantages** of viewing an organization as a system is the ability to show how external and internal forces interact to shape the organization. If management concentrates only on efficiently running the work force and ignores advances in technology that cause disruption to the work force, then competition may adopt those technologies and reduce the market share of the non-competitive manufacturer. If management is unaware of workers attitudes toward working conditions and compensation and unaware of Federal or State regulations governing working conditions they cannot operate successfully. The organization operates in a complex interrelated social setting. It must be aware of internal and external variables if it is to operate and communicate effectively. *The system model allows such an analysis of organizational communication activities.*

Communication in Organizations

Organizational effectiveness demands **effective, immediate, and appropriate communication strategies** at the point of need. Communication in todays world travels only slightly slower than the speed of light. Telephones, Fax machines, electronic mail and satellite feeds are all communication technology that allow an organization to communicate at any time to any place on the face of the globe with lightning speed. But, these advances in communication technology must be used effectively and in an appropriate manner to obtain a predetermined desired response from a specific targeted audience. Every organization must consider Internal and External audiences and communication channels if they are to be effective.

Internal Communication Systems

The internal communication networks send information inside the organizational structure (company). Some of the most common methods are memos, meetings, and rumor. Some larger corporations have adopted internal television channels to communicate within the corporation, linking widely separated geographic locations to in one satellite network. Whatever the technology employed all internal networks have some established structure.

Formal and Informal Communication

Two broad categories in internal communication networks are **formal vs. informal** channels.

Formal channels are ones approved and dictated by the organization. Informal channels are created by members of the organization to fill gaps centered by the formal organizational communication chart. Both formal and informal organizational flow can be structured and analyzed in some of the following patterns.

Network Patterns

Chain   This is the classical vertical-horizontal flow where each member of the flow communicates only with the person either immediately above or below or immediately on either side. In this flow any person in the chain can either block or facilitate communication flow.

Other Patterns of Flow   Circle, Wheel, and Y allow for a flow that passes through either a central control individual or for a flow between an individual and the immediate individuals on either side.

All of these patterns of flow contribute to centralized control but they also contribute to a slow flow and to the possibility of blocking and alteration of message.

> *Communication networks in organizations should contribute to rapid clear transmission of information with the necessary degree of control needed to accomplish the goals of the organization.*

A communication network that allows all units to communicate directly with all other units with the necessary minimum control and feedback is usually the most effective network for most organizations. Often this pattern is referred to as the **all-channel network of communication.**

These communication networks operate in both formal and informal communication within the organization.

Informal networks of communication within an organization will always exist. Quite often they are the quickest and most accurate means that the organization has to test new ideas and reactions to those ideas.

An executive in a large company knew that the janitor always checked his trash before throwing it away. He also knew that he would often hear rumors concerning ideas that he had produced in draft memo form, and then discarded, being discussed. He knew that someone in his office was gaining this information from the janitor. Therefore, he utilized this "informal channel" to test out new ideas. He would draft memos of ideas he was unsure of and throw them away. In a few days he could tell from the office talk what his department thought about those new ideas. It also served as a way to soften the blow of major changes; the employees had a few days warning before the changes occurred. All of this thanks to a janitor.

Formal lines of communication are the basic means of everyday operation in any organization. The paper work and forms that keep a company alive flow through these channels. The morning meeting or weekly briefing are essential for the communication flow in most organizations. Generally these meetings are examples of All-channel communication where department heads and their supervisor are able to communicate directly to all other department heads in the presence of the supervisor. *Formal communication channels are the official word on what is happening and what is going to happen in an organization.* It may be known through informal communication channels that the plant is going to move, but until the OFFICIAL MEMO is circulated it is not official. Generally, the more effectively an organization communicates through the formal channels the less rumor and suspicion will be generated by informal channels.

External Communication Systems

External communication networks are all lines of communication that extend beyond the organization and flow into the organization from outside sources. These communication connections are represented by any member of the organization that interacts with the outside environment.

A lobbyist or company representative are good examples of members of the organization whose job it is to deal with external communication. **For any organization to be successful they must communicate effectively with their outside audiences and potential support groups.**

Advertising, Sales, Labor-relations, Government-relations, and interaction with other organizations in the field are areas where external channels are of vital importance. An organization must be aware of the changing variables in their area of interest and interact with the external groups and forces that can mean success or failure for the organization. A misreading of the American consumer preferences in automobiles concerning size and quality was not addressed by most American auto manufacturers in the late 1970's and early 1980's. They failed to communicate effectively with external audiences. As a result they lost a significant share of the market to foreign competition.

External communication allows an organization to see and respond to external threats and opportunities.

Organizational Environment

Organizational environment refers to the *general atmosphere affecting an organization internally and externally at any given point in time.* Each organization is unique in its creation and growth. Therefore, no two organizations have the same history and organizational environment to guide them in decisions and planning. For example, the organizational environment for Toyota and Nissan reflects the unique characteristics of the Japanese culture. As a result, some of the philosophy, organizational structure and communication strategies that work in that environment may be transferable to the American setting; *but, not all of those organizational strategies will work in the American organizational environment.* Organizational Communication, like Public Speaking, Small-group Communication, and Interviewing must analyze the audience and social setting. Only after those variables have been considered can effective communication strategies be developed to accomplish specific goals.

There are several key terms involved in studies of Organizational environments.

Organizational Climate refers to the general feelings and attitudes present in the workplace. Is the climate tense and competitive or relaxed and easy-going?

Organizational Themes are ideas that an organization believes in and acts upon. Churches, Political parties, and corporations develop their basic themes (ISSUES/AGENDA) and constantly utilize them in their communication strategies.

Organizational Heroes and Myths are utilized by many organizations. The Ford Motor Company idolizes Henry Ford I and his ideas. The Democratic Party idolizes Jefferson, Jackson, Roosevelt, Truman, and Kennedy. The Republican Party idolizes Lincoln, Eisenhower, and Reagan. There are anecdotes and myths surrounding all of these men and they still influence policy, issues, and communication strategies of these organizations.

Organizational communication strategies must consider and adapt to the organizational environment in which they operate.

Remember

- Organizational effectiveness demands effective, immediate, and appropriate communication strategies at the point of need.
- Every organization must consider internal and external audiences if they are to be effective.
- Communication networks in organizations should contribute to rapid clear transmission of information with the necessary degree of control needed to accomplish the goals of the organization.